Also by Ron Felber

THE INDIAN POINT CONSPIRACY

DEATH MISSION: HAVANA

THE BLUE ICE AFFAIR

BLOOD ULTIMATUM

SEARCHERS: A TRUE STORY

# THE PRIVACY WAR

# THE PRIVACY WAR

## ONE CONGRESSMAN,
## J. EDGAR HOOVER
## AND THE FIGHT FOR THE FOURTH AMENDMENT

## BY RON FELBER

CROCE PUBLISHING GROUP

Published by Croce Publishing Group, LLC
PO Box 339
Montvale, NJ 07645-0339
www.crocepublishing.com

Please send all queries to info@crocepublishing.com.

Library of Congress Cataloging-in-Publication Data
Felber, Ron.
  The privacy war : One Congressman, J. Edgar Hoover
and the fight for the Fourth Amendment / by Ron Felber.
  p. cm.
Includes bibliographical references and index.
  ISBN 0-9719538-9-9 (pbk. : alk. paper)
  1. Gallagher, Cornelius E. 2. Legislators--United States--Biography.
  3. United States. Congress. House--Biography. 4. Privacy, Right
of--United States--History--20th century.
  5. Civil rights--UnitedStates--History--20th century. I. Title.
  E748.G144F45 2003
  328.73'092--dc21
  2002012126

Printed in the United States of America
10  9  8  7  6  5  4  3  2  1

To William Peter Blatty,
who showed me that wondrous things can happen.

# CONTENTS

The right of the people to be secure in their persons, houses, papers, and effects, against unreasonable searches and seizures, shall not be violated, and no warrants shall issue, but upon probable cause, supported by oath or affirmation, and particularly describing the place to be searched, and the persons or things to be seized.

- Amendment IV, The Bill of Rights

Much of the information in this book has been gathered from exclusive taped interviews between author Ron Felber and former congressman Cornelius E. Gallagher, which were conducted in New Jersey from December of 1998 to June of 1999.

# THE PRIVACY WAR

# FOREWORD

I first met Cornelius "Neil" Gallagher, former congressman of New Jersey's 13th District from 1958 to 1972, on December 18, 1998, through our mutual friend, Tony Ward. The idea was for me to interview him for a novel I was planning to write that involved governmental abuses of power, but it soon evolved into something much different and far more exciting.

Through our conversations, I'd learned of Gallagher's friendship with John and Robert Kennedy, his controversial relationship with the colorful lawyer Roy Cohn, his alleged connections with reputed organized crime figure Joseph "Bayonne" Zicarelli and his years in prison with E. Howard Hunt, Egil Krogh and other members of the Watergate Plumbers. What I didn't know was the story behind his sensational fall from grace or the profound effect he had on American society as we know it today regarding his thirty-year fight to protect our Fourth Amendment to the Constitution, the freedom of the individual from unreasonable governmental search and seizure.

Gallagher had been a powerful force in national politics in the 1960s and 1970s, ranking high on John Kennedy's personal list of the best and brightest. Tall and rangy, he looked like Jimmy Stewart then, and rising up as he did from working-class stock, the imagination needn't stretch far to see him as a Mr. Smith going to Washington. His body was all angles and bone, his mind a cauldron of ideals and post-World War II moxie that led the *New York Times* to name him one of Congress' five most influential legislators, eventually becoming a short list contender for vice president on the Lyndon Johnson ticket in 1964.

By all accounts, his early life read like an American dream: varsity baseball and basketball in college, family man, law school valedictorian and war hero who returned from Patton's Third Army with a Bronze Star, three Purple Hearts and a Combat Infantry Badge, taking enough time to open a thriving law practice, only to re-up with the onset of the Korean War.

But one then had to ask what went wrong. More to the point, why, when I mentioned him to a fellow author, a man from his hometown and generation, did he warn me to stay away from the man, that being anywhere near him would only cause me trouble? Trouble with what? Trouble with whom? Our first meeting would hint at many possibilities, but answer few.

His house was situated in a compound surrounded by the homes of his daughters. Still handsome, he looked like the ghost of an Irish poet. His face was ruddy with his white hair swept back to camouflage the mottle of cancer on the back of his head. A collection of photographs sat atop a baby grand piano in his living room. Among them were pictures of him with Martin Luther King Jr.; Robert Kennedy; former Louisiana Congressman and friend Hale Boggs; Indira Ghandi; Benigno Simeon "Ninoy" Aquino Jr., chief opposition leader during the era of martial law in the Philippines; John F. Kennedy; and Malcolm Little, better known as Malcolm X.

"Quite a collection of photos you have here," I remarked. "But will you please do me a favor. Don't put a picture of me on your piano top. It seems like just about every one of them has been murdered. All except you."

He answered without thinking. "Yes I am. I am dead. They just didn't do it with a bullet through my head."[1]

It was only later, after hundreds of hours of taped interviews, exhaustive research into congressional archives and careful study of recently released White House recordings from the Kennedy, Johnson and Nixon presidencies that the true context of Gallagher's destruction as a politician and a man was visible.

In August 1968, *Life* magazine published an article titled "The Congressman and the Hoodlum," alleging political ties between Gallagher and the New Jersey Mafia. It was the first in a series of Gallagher exposés, which were later described by Pulitzer Prize-winning journalist Anthony Summers as "the most savage attack on a government official in the twentieth century."[2]

At the time, Gallagher, a Democrat, was a key member of the House Committee on Foreign Affairs and Government Operations Committee, chairman of the U.S. and Canadian Interparliamentary Group, and a U.S. delegate to the Nuclear Disarmament Committee. A short four years later, he was out of Congress, had resigned as an attorney, and was a convicted felon serving the first of two stints in federal prison. His name and the effects of his landmark work on the issue of the Fourth Amendment were forever wiped clean from the slate of history.

Soon after our first meeting, my idea for a novel was eclipsed by this story, which seemed far more important to my life and those of millions of Americans. Here was a nonfiction documentary crackling with political intrigue, assassination and Mafia chieftains who were complicit with officials at the highest levels of government, the most prominent of them all being J. Edgar Hoover, director of the FBI from 1924 until his death in 1972. More important, after the terrorist attacks of September 11, 2001, Gallagher's story seemed to me a stepping stone in modern America's attempt to establish a balance between national security and individual freedom in a time of precarious international relations.

From my five years researching the book, I learned that

despite Justice Oliver Wendell Holmes' 1919 ruling in *United States v. Schenck* that "clear and present danger" must be present before freedom could be limited with all convictions upheld, 2,000 individuals were prosecuted for printing brochures and newsletters encouraging resistance to the World War I draft. I learned that during the Red Scare of the 1920s, the federal government engaged in mass deportation of aliens and two-thirds of the states passed laws prohibiting the advocacy of criminal anarchy. I also learned that during World War II, following the internment of Japanese-Americans, federal agencies began prosecuting leaders of the Communist Party USA with Senator Joseph McCarthy carrying on his famous hearings, which accused named and unnamed government officials, writers and others of Communist ties. Now, in the aftermath of September 11, 2001, Gallagher asks, Will we in the new millennium respond to fear in the same way that we did in the millennium past?

Today, Gallagher notes, anyone willing to spend time on the Internet or a few dollars with the credit-reporting service Equifax can gather more information on an individual than all of Hitler's Gestapo or Stalin's KGB ever could. FBI agents using the Carnivore diagnostic tool monitor cell phones, e-mail and even ATM transactions. The ESCHELON spying system of the National Security Agency (NSA) gives intelligence operatives access to every electronic communication in the world, intercepting messages by the billions per hour, violating the privacy of American citizens and foreign nationals virtually unchallenged.

One reads in the paper about the U.S. Commission on National Security/21st Century calling for the creation of a National Homeland Security Agency in an effort to combat terrorist attacks on U.S. soil. In Washington, D.C., federal law enforcement agencies proposed mandatory blood sampling of civilians in order to create DNA profiles on every American citizen. How did we arrive at this point? Will anyone question the authority of those who will craft the post-September 11 America?

In writing this book, I looked to the past to find the answers to our future. Had anyone dared to confront the awesome power of America's federal agencies in control of our freedom before? The answers to these questions, I would learn, resided with Gallagher who, for the first time in his seventy-nine years, was willing to share the story of his incredible journey behind the curtain of the American government.

# THE PRIVACY WAR

**RON FELBER**

# I
# The Raid

### Columbia, N.J., February 6, 1992

It was early on a Wednesday morning. From the kitchen window, Gallagher's wife, Rick, observed two unmarked cars pulling onto the long dirt road leading to the ridge where the family's homes were nestled. She was baby-sitting Patti and Bridget's brood of preschoolers, and though it seemed early for guests, people were always coming by these days, if not to visit one of their daughters, then to visit Gallagher, recovering now from his shattered career. Only a week before a reporter from the *New York Post* dropped by to interview him about Oliver Stone's new film *JFK*, since Gallagher had been friends with the president. And over the past month, he'd entertained requests from several universities to lecture on the issue of privacy and the Fourth Amendment. Equally encouraging, his fellow citizens were urging him to run for Congress again despite the fact that he was now in his seventies.

Rick thought little of the cars and returned to the children. But they then converged like wasps, she remembers. Two cars became four; four became eight; eight became sixteen, until they were soon swarmed. Then there was a knock, but before answering she took a final look outside. She was stunned. Seventeen cars, all unmarked, arrived at their house. And they were still coming.

**25**

The agents began to advance on the adjacent homes of their daughters. Some were FBI. Some were IRS. Some were DEA. Rick hurried to the door, her eyes darting to the staircase, frantic that Gallagher was still asleep and her ninety-four-year old mother, who'd been ill, would be forced to leave the house. And the kids: Kevin, Lauren, Matthew and Caitlin. No matter what happened, she told herself, she wouldn't be afraid. Fear is their game, Gallagher had told her over the years.

"Mrs. Claire Gallagher?" the special agent demanded, holding a piece of paper in his hand as the second agent raised a badge. A third agent, a woman, trained a gun on her. "We have a warrant to search these premises," the first agent explained as he ordered his partner to block the door. Rick then realized that there were no fewer than fifty agents waiting behind him, many brandishing pistols, rifles or shotguns. "Where's your husband?" he demanded. "Where's his office?"

"We have young children here," Rick pleaded. "Can't you at least wait until I get them?"

The special agent appraised seventy-year-old Rick, standing in her robe. "Get him," he relented. "We'll wait here with the door open."

Rick flew up the staircase and said a quick Our Father as she entered their bedroom. Knowing how upset he'd be, she feared her husband would have a heart attack. She had to stay calm, she told herself.

"What? What is it?" Gallagher asked frantically.

"It's the police, Neil, or the FBI, or both. But they have a search warrant."

"What are you talking about?" he exploded. Rick begged him to try to reason with them but it was too late. He ran down the stairs. "You better have a goddamned warrant," he demanded before reaching the bottom step, ordering the agent to show identification and official papers, which the agent did.

Gallagher studied the warrant and shook his head. It accused him of money laundering, illegal possession of drugs and illegal possession of firearms. "Are you people out your minds?"

The agent didn't bother to reply, and with his gesture of a Calvary officer, others stormed in.

"There's a sick woman up there," Rick hollered after them, but when they came upon her mother's locked door, they kicked it in.

"What is the matter with you?" she cried. "That's an old woman in there. Do you want to kill her? She's been ill for weeks." Rick tugged at the agent's arm in vain.

"Get her out of here," he ordered his partner. "Take her downstairs or I'll have her arrested." They stood with their hands on their guns.

"It's okay, Mom," Rick cried as the agent escorted her out while other teams moved up the stairs and into the attic. "Everything will be all right," she whispered to herself. "Just do as they tell you. Do as they say."

Gallagher then came up the stairs.

"Where are the children?" Rick demanded.

"It's okay, Rick," Gallagher said. "They're here with me."

He had stayed calm, Rick noticed, calmer perhaps than she, with Kevin, Lauren, Matthew and Caitlin clinging to him. The dresser drawers were pulled off their tracks, the contents dumped on the floor. Closets were emptied, files scattered and sofas stripped in search of hidden cash, drugs or weapons, which weren't there. Through it all, Rick remembers, he stayed calm.

Gallagher could have guessed something like this would happen. What he could not know was that this investigation stemmed from an FBI/DEA/IRS probe begun nine years earlier and reinitiated by the assistant federal prosecutor in 1984. Accused of international drug trafficking and money laundering, Gallagher's phone would be tapped and family members put under surveillance for a decade.

This day, however, Gallagher had to take it, eyes leveled, angry and humiliated. As he sat at the foot of his staircase, he was forced to idly watch as his home and the homes of his daughters were ransacked. It just didn't seem to end, he agonized. It wouldn't end until he was dead like his friends Hale Boggs, the Kennedys and Martin Luther King.

He looked up at the special agent.

"I was ordered to personally see that nothing's taken from your home that the warrant doesn't call for," the agent said.

"That warrant is written so broadly you could take anything you want. I don't have to tell you that."

"We do what we can."

"And how about now? How do I know you or any one of your agents isn't going to drop a bag of cocaine or heroin in my desk drawer?"

The agent's eyes were not so jovial anymore. "I guess you're just going to have to trust us, Congressman."

## II
## Humble Beginnings

**"The funeral was the largest ever held in Hudson County."**

The program for an Armistice Day celebration held October 21, 1926, in Bayonne featured the reading of John McCrae's World War I poem "In Flanders Field" and a keynote address by Neil Gallagher, Sr. of Leddy Post. Gallagher the Junior was only five years old, but he fondly recalls that day and others like it when his father, the most decorated veteran in the city's history, would make a speech or lead a parade. Gallagher has few memories of his father, but some of the most vivid relate to those parades.

Still, these were anything but easy days. When Gallagher's father returned from World War I, he'd been awarded a Distinguished Service Cross, a French Croix de Guerre and an Italian Medal of Honor, but he came back wounded. A machine gunner sergeant in the 309th Machine Gun Company of the 78th Division, he'd been shot in the lung and nearly had his arm blown off at Château-Thierry during a brutal German attack on American trenches. Regardless, he stayed at his post, machine gun blazing. The Germans were using mustard gas at the time, and he was exposed to it. It was this that kept him in and out of veteran's hospitals for the eight years that he survived.

Gallagher's father and mother were married after Neil Sr.'s

return from the war. Gallagher Jr.'s brother Jack, two years his junior, served in Africa and Italy in the 34th Infantry Division. After World War I, Neil Sr. returned to Bayonne to a hero's welcome. He was appointed to the Bayonne police department and later rose to detective, a position he held until he died in 1929 as a result of his wounded lung and exposure to mustard gas. The funeral was the largest ever held in Hudson County.[1]

Making ends meet wasn't easy for the Gallaghers and many others during the 1930s as the Great Depression plied its way into the lives of nearly all Americans. Unemployment lines grew but, on a county level, Jersey City mayor Frank Hague's ability to "deliver the vote" for Franklin Roosevelt was rewarded with enormous largess. Hague, not a governor or senator, cleared all federal patronage jobs. Roosevelt's aide, Harry Hopkins, gave Hague control over 1,800 Civil Works Administration jobs and appointed Bill Ely as Head of the State's Work Progress Administration, which employed over 76,000 people.[2] Hague also controlled the distribution of Federal Emergency Relief Aid, so the burden of the times would have fallen far more heavily were it not for the Hudson County patronage system.

It was this peculiar blend of community and sharing that kept the Gallagher family afloat during that period. Neighbors pitched in during particularly tough times while Gallagher's mother worked at the veteran's hospital with Jack. Gallagher attended St. Mary's grammar school during the day and delivered the *Jersey Journal* and *Colliers* magazine after school let out. At the age of sixteen, he signed up for the Civilian Military Corps where he spent one month each summer at Ft. Dix training to be a military officer. By day, he worked at the Electro Dynamic plant in Bayonne. At night he attended John Marshall College in Jersey City on a baseball and basketball scholarship.

Two years later, with the harbingers of war heavy in the air, Gallagher volunteered for the Enlisted Reserves. Hitler had absorbed Austria and Czechoslovakia, and then invaded Poland. Japan was fighting in China. The Nazis had signed the Pact of Steel—known generally as the Axis Alliance, which later included Japan—with Italy. And despite Roosevelt's Neutrality Act, most in the military understood that the United States would eventually be drawn into the conflict. Prior to Pearl Harbor, Gallagher was on standby duty as a sergeant in the enlisted reserves. He was later commissioned a 2nd Lieutenant and assigned to the 80th Division, which became part of General Patton's Third Army. On December 8, 1941, the day following the attack on Pearl Harbor, Gallagher and thousands of other American soldiers were on their way to war in Europe.

Twenty-two months later, while stationed at Fort Benning, Georgia, he married Claire "Rick" Richter, his high-school sweetheart. Rick's father, Al, the son of a German immigrant, was a carpet layer for Macy's in New York. Her mother, Siena, whose parents had also immigrated, raised Rick and her older brother and sister, while tending to their modest home just five blocks from where Gallagher was born and raised. The following year, Gallagher was leading a rifle company through Nazi-occupied France.

On August 18, 1944, the 80th was in the Battle of Argentan-Falaise Gap. At 0800, the 2nd Battalion started up the Argentan-Trum Road. The 1st Battalion advancing on Argentan had been pinned down by enemy fire. Brigadier General E.W. Searby asked Lt. Gallagher to take four men on a patrol to locate the enemy. The general went along and they located a German tank in a hedgerow to the north of Argentan. When the patrol opened fire, the tank withdrew and two machine guns supporting it opened fire on the general, Gallagher and his men. General Searby started toward one of the machine guns. Gallagher prevailed upon the general to give him the honor, which he did reluctantly. The men covered his advance while Gallagher knocked out both machine guns and wounded the tank commander who was visible in the turret. The battalion moved up in support of the 1st.

Later that morning when the fog lifted, the 3rd Battalion was caught suddenly in an open field. When Lt. Col. Lindell stood up and yelled to get the troops moving, he was hit. Gallagher and a fellow officer got the troops in hand after they had been under heavy attack by the German tanks. They then reported to Lt. Col. Golden that they were ready to counter-attack. During the battle for Argentan, according to J.J. Broderick, "Lt. Gallagher was running around taking grenades from everyone and throwing them like baseballs, knocking out machine guns and a tank." He was cited on the spot by General McBride.

Other action followed including the capture of the headquarters of a German division and more than two hundred prisoners by a patrol he was leading. But it wasn't until later that year, as Patton's Third Army rolled beyond the now German Alsace to the German border, that Gallagher suffered a fateful injury.

They were on their way into Germany. General Abrams, then a light colonel, was commanding a tank battalion to which his rifle company was attached. At the time, they would run up 120 miles and behind German lines when a political decision was made to deny Patton the gas needed to move the Third Army forward. Of course, the situation seemed incredible to them. In their view, they could have gone straight through to Berlin since the Germans were falling back so rapidly that they couldn't organize a counterattack. In the midst of this mammoth reorganization, Gallagher, working from a vehicle steeped in burning equipment, was rocked when a nearby German ammunition truck exploded. The truck was thrown in the air, and by the time it crashed to the ground, Gallagher had taken shrapnel in his right arm and lower back.

Promoted to company commander for valor in action, he received eight decorations including three Purple Hearts, a Bronze Star and Presidential Citation. After a short stint in an infantry field hospital, he was transported over the channel to Oxford, England, where he was to recover, that is, until Britain's disastrous Red Devil engagement. Owing to a shortage of hospital space, he was sent back to the States where he spent six months recovering from his wounds at an army hospital in Ozark, Alabama.

In February 1945, Gallagher was discharged from the hospital and reassigned from the pool of wounded infantry officers to the position of honor guard for President Roosevelt in Hyde Park, New York. Recently returned from his historic conference at Yalta with Churchill and Stalin, the president was in failing health. He died on April 12 of that year. This caused a last-minute change in Gallagher's assignment and he became assistant professor of Military Science back home in New Jersey at Rutgers University. Soon after, Gallagher assumed the role of professor/student, teaching classes by day and attending John Marshall Law School by night.

Times were buoyant for everyone, it seemed. With the war in Europe over, the temperament of the entire country had changed. True, 1945 was the year Nazi war crimes came to light and the widening influence of Stalin's Soviet Union seemed more than a little troublesome. But the U.S. had the bomb to leverage with, which left most Americans ready to let loose and enjoy their newfound prosperity.

But if 1945 was a good year, 1947 was a great one for Gallagher and Rick because this was the year Rick gave birth to their first daughter, Diane. It was also the year Gallagher received his honorable discharge and graduated valedictorian from John Marshall.

Soon following, Frank Hague's predecessor, John Kenny, and the Hudson County organization gave Gallagher his first taste of politics. Kenny encouraged him to run for Freeholder once he'd established a successful law practice and helped found a group, along with friend Bill McGraw, called the Young Democrats. But it was not to be. On June 25, 1950, the Soviet-equipped North Korean People's Army crossed the 38th parallel into the Republic of South Korea fighting the U.S.-equipped South Korean army. With a shortage of infantry officers, the reserve pool needed to be tapped. In early September of that year, Rick handed him a telegram that had arrived that morning. It was a processing notice from the War Department ordering Gallagher to report to Yokohama for active duty in ten days.

That night Gallagher attended a conference where Kenny was to announce the slate of candidates for Bayonne freeholder. Kenny pulled him aside and told him that he wanted to announce him for the position. Gallagher told him about the telegram.

"But I thought you were on disability?" Kenny asked.

"I am, forty percent. I get a VA pension."

"Well, we'll just see about that," Kenny said and marched over to a telephone booth where he called Secretary of the Army Archibald Alexander.

"No, no," Gallagher pleaded with him, taking hold of the phone. "With all due respect, Mayor, I'm getting a little too old to dodge the draft. If they need retreads like me this must be a pretty serious war."

In February 1952, after serving one year, Gallagher was retired from the army for physical disability. That same year, Rick gave birth to their second daughter, Christine. This occasion marked a change in temperament for both he and Rick since he pledged to her that he'd begin using some of his new contacts to start building his law practice and run for office, believing that the young men of his generation had to begin taking the reins of the country. He'd get no argument from Rick, who'd been holding the family together in his absence on a financial shoestring.

Still, the reward for his efforts came sooner than anyone could have anticipated. After taking up Kenny's offer and serving one term as freeholder, Gallagher became commissioner of the New Jersey Turnpike Authority and was voted a delegate to the Democratic National Convention. He arrived in Chicago as the de facto leader of the new statewide Young Democrats, with experience in elected office and a staunch following.

The convention, held on August 13, 1956, at the Chicago Convention Center, seemed straightforward enough. Adlai Stevenson, former governor of Illinois and the Democratic candidate for president, was the frontrunner for the nomination. The only question was, who would be his running mate?

The New Jersey delegation milled around the floor, and reporters interviewed Hubert Humphrey, Senator Estes Kefauver from Tennessee and the young Jack Kennedy, senator from Massachusetts. By the time Gallagher arrived, however, there was a palpable change in the dynamics of the selection for the second spot on the ticket. Doubtless, it had a lot to do with Kennedy's recent appearance on *Face the Nation*, but there was more going on than that. The issue of Communism persisted, as witnessed in the anti-Soviet revolutions and subsequent put-downs in Poland and Hungary that year and the raging guerrilla war being fought by Fidel Castro against the Batista government in Cuba.

Yet, at home, where the gross national product had grown from $167 billion in 1945 to $400 billion in 1955,[3] prosperity had created a dubious sense of security that played itself out in television shows like *Father Knows Best*. But with the rise of Elvis Presley in music, Marlon Brando in his portrayal of a motorcycle gang leader in *The Wild One* and James Dean in his role as an angry, directionless youth in *Rebel Without A Cause*, Gallagher was beginning to see a less naive America. As he would find out, this change would also surface in American politics.

RON FELBER

# III
# The Seeds of Popularity

**"The next time Kennedy and he met,
Gallagher would be a congressman."**

Over the coming years as his popularity grew, Gallagher would
find himself associating with individuals both noteworthy and
notorious: John and Bobby Kennedy, Gerry Ford, Lyndon
Johnson, Hubert Humphrey, Joe Zicarelli, Bill Colby, Shirley
MacLaine, Catherine Deneuve, J. Edgar Hoover, Allen Dulles and,
most frequently, Roy Cohn, chief counsel to Joe McCarthy during
his Senate hearings.

It was at a dinner in June 1954, at the Waldorf-Astoria in
Manhattan when Gallagher first met Cohn. Invited by Federal
District Judge James Coolihan, Gallagher recoiled when he heard
that Cohn would be there. Around this time, Joe McCarthy, though
still in the Senate, had been censured and Cohn, who still had his
defenders, had left the McCarthy-Army hearings with a reputation
for the basest kind of manipulation and ruthlessness. "Why would I
want to go to a dinner with Cohn even in the room?" Gallagher
argued, having boycotted McCarthy to a storm of Catholic criticism
at a communion breakfast five years before. But Coolihan explained
a legal situation in New Jersey that Cohn needed Gallagher's help
with and that how a friendship with the man could give him high-

profile contacts who could help him enormously in the political playing field. Gallagher thought of his meager bank account, his new home and daughter and reluctantly agreed.

Cohn was the rich, twenty-seven-year-old son of a New York supreme court justice, Jewish and fanatically right-wing. Gallagher was the working-class, thirty-three-year-old son of an Irish Catholic policeman and a burgeoning civil libertarian. Despite their differences, they had two things in common: ambition and youth, and that evening at dinner they hit it off.

The legal situation at hand, Gallagher soon came to find out, involved a New Jersey magazine distribution company, which was being sued along with its board that included several high flyers for distribution of pornography. Cohn was general counsel of the company and was on its board. Since the case was being tried in New Jersey the board wanted an attorney from the state to handle it. And since Gallagher was a major proponent of free speech, Cohn thought Gallagher would be perfect for the job. In the end, Gallagher proved to be a good business partner. He won the case, but more important, made an influential contact. He didn't bill Cohn for that one, and from then on, Cohn let him handle all his New Jersey overspill. This was the beginning of what proved to be an interesting friendship.

Through the years Cohn was an enigma to the congressman. The notorious lawyer is remembered mostly as the rabid anti-Communist of the McCarthy hearings, mercilessly destroying the careers of witnesses, many of whom simply did not agree with his views. This was a man whose hearings allegedly caused the suicides of United Nations secretariat Abe Feller and Ray Kaplan of Voice of America. He bragged about sending Julius and Ethel Rosenberg to the electric chair and, along with his mentor, Joseph McCarthy, attempted to rout suspected gays out of the State Department when he himself, it is alleged, was secretly homosexual.

Cohn's history with the House Un-American Activities Committee (HUAC) was well known, but one aspect of his life that Gallagher could never, at that time, fully comprehend was the intense personal relationship McCarthy and he had with J. Edgar Hoover, who had allegedly leaked illegally obtained information to the HUAC in order to destroy the reputations of individuals. Gallagher attests that Cohn was acting as a go-between for the FBI, sharing this information with high-profile columnists. In return, the columnists would plant nefarious stories about those whom the agency held in disfavor.

Cohn allegedly also pioneered the prosecutory techniques used during the McCarthy hearings. One tactic involved bringing suspected members, or sympathizers, of the Communist Party USA before the committee and bombarding them with questions, some related to party affiliations. But just as many questions were personal in nature. The philosophy was, the more embarrassing the questions the better, Gallagher believes. To hide a cheating wife's indiscretion or protect a loved one from unnecessary implication, according to Gallagher, HUAC attorneys attempted to manipulate high-profile witnesses into perjuring themselves, which could bring favorable headlines to the committee's work. The strategy was simple, Gallagher attests: If they couldn't put individuals in jail for what they were charged with, they'd get them for something else, usually perjury, a crime with a sentence of four to five years.

Despite Cohn's reputation, he and Gallagher became fast friends, arguing about politics, partying at Manhattan night spots like Toots Shors or the 21 Club and, generally, enjoying the excitement of the éclat with Cohn's business buddies and a stream of celebrities.

In May 1955, Cohn invited Gallagher, off the cuff, to Monte

Carlo. Another time Cohn came home from plastic surgery with stitches everywhere. The obvious question for a man who spent so much time dieting and swimming and who had facelifts as often as every two to three years was, why don't you get the scar on the bridge of your nose taken care of? "Then everybody would know that I had my face done," Cohn replied. [1]

With John F. Kennedy it was a similar story. He and Gallagher had much in common and hit it off when they first met at the Democratic National Convention in 1956. Both Irish-Catholics and in their early thirties, they'd returned from World War II as heroes, which helped catapult them into national politics.

No one better suited the persona of youthful America than Jack Kennedy: a young, Harvard-educated war hero, author, husband and family man. More, for the first time ever in American politics, at least on the national level, a man of grace entered the public domain. Kennedy was fresh. He was new. He had edge. Neither angry nor restless, he was modern and forward-looking. He spoke of change and vigor while being hip and cool, a jetsetter just back from Palm Beach or Las Vegas. He was the man of the age.

With Kennedy, there was much going on at the convention of 1956. And if it was just a feeling earlier in the day, the feeling transformed into reality that afternoon when Kennedy advisor Kenny O'Donnell came to seek Gallagher out. Kennedy had decided to make a run for the second slot and wanted to see him, he explained. They walked across the floor to the Massachusetts delegation. Kennedy was shaking hands and giving instructions to Bobby, and even his sisters, Eunice and Jean. The level of competition had turned up suddenly because the team had yet to truly organize. Gallagher walked over to Kennedy. They shook hands. It was strange, Gallagher remembers, to think of this young, skinny kid so prominent and self-assured.

O'Donnell introduced them and their conversation immediately turned to the war.

"Maybe you've heard I was in the navy," Kennedy joked, referring to all the press he'd been getting for the PT-109 patrol boat, which became a part of the Kennedy legend after he survived its sinking off the Solomon Islands in the South Pacific in 1943.

"It was the infantry for me, Jack, and that's like being a priest. Once you're in the infantry, you're in for life."

"So, aside from the war," Kennedy went on, "we seem to have a mutual interest in politics. In my opinion, it's time for men of our generation, back from the war, to have something to say about the national scene. Is that another interest we share?"

It was, but Gallagher thought for a moment, wondering if this was something Kennedy really wanted to know or was using as a way to introduce himself to delegates from all over the country for the next time around. Looking him straight in the eyes, he was convinced that if Kennedy didn't want it before, he certainly wanted it now. So Gallagher offered his help.

In the end, however, Kennedy lost to Carey Estes Kefauver. He was disappointed, of course, but losing was the best thing that could have happened to his career. Stevenson went down in flames, but the young Kennedy got national television exposure. People liked him and everyone knew that at this age he'd be back even stronger.

The same could be said about Gallagher at that time. Like Kennedy, he had ambition and a war record, and he looked the part. The next time Kennedy and he met, Gallagher would be a congressman and Kennedy would have his eye locked and unblinking on the presidency.

Gallagher's campaign to represent the 13th District in

Congress began early. Quick to remember Al Sieminski's close call in 1956 where, in a district that hadn't had a Republican winner since 1905, he barely defeated Norman Roth by 57 of the nearly 60,000 votes that had been cast. This was an attractive possibility for Gallagher who'd become inspired by the "new" politics Kennedy had described, the politics of their generation. Beyond that, if Sieminski didn't run, the hometown vote in Bayonne would surely be his, leaving him anxious to launch a strategy that argued that Bayonne plus one additional ward in Jersey City would equal victory.

Even as Gallagher continued working at his law practice, he campaigned at a furious pace, visiting industrial plants in the morning, lunching with service clubs at noon, touring supermarkets, speaking at women's clubs, and going house-to-house in the 7th Ward (the state's largest) followed by the usual Democratic political rallies in the evening. Taking a page from the Kennedy strategy book, even Rick was active hosting Gals for Gallagher campaign parties and bringing Diane, then ten, and Chrissy, four, to community centers for the local newspapers.

Key issues for his campaign were the Cold War and the conflicts in Berlin and Korea, which were important to the people of Bayonne and Jersey City. But in hindsight, Gallagher says today, the most important issue to the locals was simple trust. "People wanted to know you were a guy who would go down to Washington and do the right thing for them," he says. "These were neighborhood people. They wanted to know that you were someone who understood their problems of unemployment, poor medical care and inadequate schools. They wanted to know you were the person to come to when they needed help. It got to be a running joke around town. I was the priest and my law office was the confessional because I'd see people on Friday evenings starting at seven and continuing until one or two in the morning."

True to his word, Sieminski, the 13th District incumbent, announced that he would not seek re-election late that same year, only to recant in January. Since Jim Murray had disavowed what was left of Hague's organization by taking on Mayor Kenny and the organization's commissioners two years earlier, Gallagher received Kenny's backing, leaving Sieminski to fend for himself as an independent and Murray to run on his own victory ticket of the Hudson County Democratic Party.

As anticipated, it was a fight to the finish with Sieminski apt to play the spoiler, splitting the Bayonne vote, and Murray carrying the Irish and Italian votes in his hometown of Jersey City. But three things prevented the obvious from happening: First, Sieminski's support in Bayonne, after his vacillation on running, was negligible. Second, Gallagher's early start, coupled with the efforts of the Young Democrats, paid off and he won the 7th Ward. Third, a new minority had developed unnoticed and underrepresented until he'd made his door-to-door visits: African Americans. They liked what Gallagher had to say about the sanctity of individual rights and freedom under the Constitution, giving him nearly 90 percent of their vote.

That night, while the votes were being counted, Rick was so nervous that she wouldn't so much as crack a smile until every vote was counted and both Sieminski and Murray conceded. Gallagher gained 27,604 votes, beating James Murray by a margin of 5,876. The champagne came out and they toasted their victory.

What neither Rick nor Gallagher could know however was that with his election to Congress that day, a strange destiny had been set in motion. The next twelve months would put him in touch with the Mafia, the emerging Communist dictator of Cuba, the soon-to-be-assassinated president of the United States, a right-wing Catholic cardinal who Gallagher believes betrayed his church to curry favor with the FBI and an army of American citizens who claimed their own government was spying on them.

# IV
# The Abuse of Polygraph Testing

**"What kind of country is this where a young girl can be interrogated like a prisoner for a simple desk job?"**

The opening session of the 1958 Congress began with the swearing in of the new class. Along with Gallagher, George Bush, Republican from Texas; Dan Rostenkowski, Democrat from Michigan; and John Lindsey, Democrat from New York, raised their right hands and pledged "to support and defend the Constitution of the United States against all enemies, foreign and domestic."The gallery cheered. Rick, Diane and Chrissy enthusiastically applauded the arrival of the 86th Congress of the United States. Working fast and diligently to be part of something that could genuinely influence world events, his real ambition, he shunned membership in the powerful Ways and Means Committee, turning his sights instead to foreign affairs.

With Fidel Castro in Cuba, average citizens building bomb shelters in their backyards and *Sputnik* circling the globe, Gallagher had to decide what he was going to give and when. But given the world situation, who could have predicted that a young girl would link him to a chain of events that would change his life forever?

It was after hours. He'd been working late in his office in the Old Congressional Building and was about to leave when he heard a woman screaming. She was stopped by a security officer. Gallagher went to the vestibule. She was middle-aged, holding her daughter, about seventeen, by the arm. Both were obviously upset and the daughter was sobbing.

"I want to see a congressman!" the mother shouted. "I want to see a congressman this minute!"

Gallagher walked over to her. "Which congressman would you like to see?"

"I don't care! Any!"

Gallagher invited she and her daughter into his office. Gertrude Miller was her name, and once they became comfortable she insisted that her daughter, Theresa, a recent high-school graduate, recount what happened to her that afternoon during an interview for a receptionist position at the Department of Interior.

"I filled out my application for the job," Theresa began reluctantly. "After some questions, I was asked to go into another room where they told me I would have to take a lie-detector test. The woman brought me into a room that had no windows, but a mirror that was set in the wall. There was a table, two chairs and this machine that was built into the table, which had straps and wires attached. A young man, who was waiting for me, told me to sit. I sat across from him, and he put the straps on me and sat down, not facing me because my chair faced the mirror. Then, he started asking me questions, working the dials on the machine as I answered.

"The first questions were simple," she continued with embarrassment, "like where I lived and about my family and school. I answered, but he never looked at me. He was always staring at the machine.

"The questions then became more difficult like 'What political groups do you belong to?' I said, 'None. I'm too young to vote.'

Theresa's chin began to quiver as she looked at her mother. Then he asked me, 'Who do you sleep with?' 'I sleep with myself,' I said. 'Who do you have sex with?' 'No one,' I said, but he kept asking."

Theresa glanced again at her mother, now sobbing. She continued. "Then he said, 'You must have sex with someone. Do you sleep with other women? Are you a lesbian? Why are you lying?' That's when I started to cry. He began screaming at me, so I tore off the straps and ran home."

Theresa shook her head violently. "I knew I could never get the job after that," she cried. "I knew that I'd done something stupid and when I got home, I told my mother. When she heard it, she got very angry and took me downstairs to get a cab and come here."

Gertrude put her hand on her daughter's wrist for comfort. "What kind of country is this where a young girl can be interrogated like a prisoner for a simple desk job, Congressman?" Gertrude cried.

That night Gallagher called his staff, amazed at what he'd heard, thinking all the while about his daughters and the potential for them to be abused in such a way. "What about her right to privacy?" he demanded of his staff. "Why would polygraph tests be given to a prospective receptionist in a non-sensitive position in the Department of Interior? Who authorizes practices like this? Who pays for them? What's done with the resulting information? Is it possible that the questions asked be standardized? Or was this man simply using those questions as a means of intimidation, exercising some perverse personal power over women like Theresa Miller?"

He asked these same questions again that very night in tens of letters he sent to the secretaries of the Departments of Interior, State, Defense, Commerce and thirty-four additional agencies. The response was shocking: No one at the top levels of those organizations, other than the CIA, FBI and Department of Defense, was aware of the testing. The reason was that only mid-level government employees were using funds appropriated for other areas to finance the testing. There was no standardization for the tests. The training required of the tester, as in the Theresa Miller case, consisted only of a high-school diploma and a two-week course given at Camp Gordon Army Base in Atlanta, Georgia.

At Gallagher's urging, several agencies that year agreed to abandon the practice of polygraph testing as a means of routine personnel screening for non-sensitive positions, but most would refuse. In Gallagher's opinion, the victory was Pyrrhic. There was more to the issue of testing, more than he could ever have imagined. When he subsequently pushed for the creation of a congressional subcommittee to investigate this issue of privacy, he was warned by several congressmen that he could be in serious trouble if he got too deeply involved.

It would be a long time before Gallagher understood exactly what their warnings meant. Given the benefit of hindsight, today he wonders how much anyone in Congress knew about the abuse by government that had been raging for years. At the time, did they know, as Gallagher would later discover, that many of their fellow congressman, especially those involved in oversight committees of the FBI, were being blackmailed by J. Edgar Hoover? At the time, did they know that many of their private phones and offices and even the caucus rooms of the Old Congressional Building were bugged? These invasions of privacy, as well as devastatingly more serious secret government operations, Gallagher would soon learn, were legion.

# V
# Before the Bay of Pigs

**"Juana admitted to him that Castro was in league with the Soviets."**

In May, 1959, Gallagher received an interesting phone call. It was Joe Zicarelli. As his was a household name in 1950s Bayonne, Gallagher had heard of Zicarelli, an alleged crime boss who ran the numbers and gambling operations throughout Hudson County.

"You know, Congressman, people think just because guys like me are in the business we are in that we can't be patriots, but I am a patriot and I want to prove it. I came in contact with a guy who knows Castro in Cuba."

Zicarelli then told Gallagher about Lou Raino, a man who was close to Castro. Raino, Zicarelli claimed, had information that he thought Gallagher, as a member of the Foreign Affairs Committee, would be interested in.

"What kind of information?"

"No way, Congressman. This is big. This is about national security. Not over the phone."

Gallagher agreed to meet Raino the following morning in his office. Raino explained that he had been living in Cuba with Castro; Castro's brother, Raul; and Che Guevera in the Sierra Maestra Mountains for eighteen months before the takeover. His girlfriend, Juana, was Fidel's sister. He was like part of the family, he claimed.

Raino went on to explain how he originally admired the leader, but became disenchanted with him after Juana admitted to him that Castro was in league with the Soviets. More, Raino claimed to have later seen Soviet engineers surveying the island for missile sites to be aimed at the United States. He said that he'd even spoken with Soviet officers who told him that the operation had been planned since before the takeover and that construction was beginning on the actual missile silos now that Castro was in power. This was the beginning, according to Raino, of what ultimately became the Cuban Missile Crisis. He claimed to know where the missiles were located and even the names of the Soviet officers involved.

"I love America," said Raino. "I fought in World War II and feel obligated to speak with someone at the CIA."

For Gallagher, this was, needless to say, hard to believe. Yet, with the Cold War, intercontinental missiles, air-raid shelters and possible nuclear war hot topics of the times, Gallagher couldn't turn his back on the man. So he called Richard Bissell, deputy director of the CIA under Allen Dulles.

They met in Gallagher's office the next morning. Bissell sat across from them. He offered Raino a cigarette, lit one himself and flicked on a portable tape recorder. Raino explained to Bissell what he'd told Gallagher and that he'd been living in Cuba since 1956. He met Juana while working at a hotel in Santiago through a mutual friend. Later in their relationship, Juana told Raino about a deal between Castro and Nikita Sergeyevich Khrushchev, which negotiated a cooperation between them for the defense of Cuba in the event of aggression. The deal involved the planting of medium- and intermediate-range ballistic missile launchers each with nuclear warheads and surface-to-air missile batteries. Juana, he said, called her brother the Antichrist. "He trusts her and he is a braggart," said Raino.

"Suppose this is all true?" Gallagher said, but Bissell didn't see that as a possibility. Bissell explained that they had a number of operatives in Cuba who would have picked up on this already. Worse, he seemed convinced that Raino was a Mafia operative who'd been running guns to Castro and simply couldn't be trusted.

"Listen," Raino said. "I'll volunteer to go back there. Give me a camera or a tape recorder and I'll talk to the Russian engineers. I'll take pictures of the sites, and I don't want any money to do it. I'm a veteran. I'm a patriot."

Bissell was unconvinced, leaving Gallagher feeling that the intelligence community was shunning a wealth of knowledge. Bissell did, however, set up a meeting for Gallagher and Raino at FBI headquarters in Washington, but the same thing happened. The authorities there simply didn't believe their source and ultimately sent Lou Raino a letter thanking him for his time, which left both he and Gallagher dumbfounded: Wasn't the government even a little concerned about the possibility of nuclear weaponry just miles off U.S. soil?

Given the astounding lack of interest in information about a situation that would bring the United States to the brink of nuclear war just three years later, Gallagher took his story and his credentials as a member of the House Foreign Affairs Committee to Arthur Sylvester, a Princeton scholar on the subject of Soviet affairs, who was the Washington editor of the *Newark Evening News*. The result of that meeting was a headline article appearing in the February 7, 1960, edition of the paper outlining the situation.

Shortly after, several stories surfaced asserting that the missile silos were, in fact, being created at the time of Raino's statements. In addition, the name and description of a KGB agent working under diplomatic cover in Cuba at that time were ultimately identified. Finally, Robert McNamara would appoint

Arthur Sylvester to Assistant Secretary of State to explain the Cuban Missile Crisis to the American public in a live television press conference held at the height of the confrontation.

# VI
# The Rising Stars

**"'Peace, Prosperity, Progress. In the end,
that's what it's all about, isn't it?'"**

On January 1, 1960, Gallagher met John Kennedy and his aides
Kenny O'Donnell and Larry O'Brien at the Carlyle Hotel in New
York City. The following morning he would be endorsing Jack's
candidacy in the House Caucus Room. Four days later Kennedy,
himself, would be formally announcing. Spirits were high among
the group with Mayor Kenny, who was now an established power-
broker in Eastern Democratic politics, actively supporting
Kennedy's run.

When Gallagher entered Kennedy's suite, O'Donnell and
O'Brien greeted him. Kennedy, smiling broadly, handsome and
suntanned as usual, clapped both of his hands over Gallagher's.

"Good to see you, Neil. How's life in Hudson County?"

"Life's good, Jack. It seems like Hudson County and all of
New Jersey's fast becoming Kennedy Country."

"Come, sit down," he laughed. "Drink?"

"No thanks." He saw that O'Brien and O'Donnell, who were
already sitting, seemed all business.

"I'm excited about tomorrow. So is Mayor Kenny. He's running around Jersey City like a twenty-year-old."

"It's not Kenny that concerns us, Neil," O'Donnell shot back. "It's the governor. July will be here sooner than any of us imagine. We're hoping he'll change his mind about favorite son status by the time the convention rolls around."

"Bob's a great guy but stubborn. I think he believes he has a chance."

"You're joking," said O'Brien, not so pleasantly.

"No, I mean it. But look, Mayor Kenny may be able to help and I'll see what I can do. As I'll make clear tomorrow, we need a strong national candidate, not Meyner to whip Nixon in November."

O'Brien was about to take it up a notch when Kennedy cut him off. "If Neil says he'll look into it, that's good enough for me. You know, coming so early, your endorsement means a lot. I appreciate it and want to thank you personally. It's also my opinion that this campaign is going to be a real ball breaker. Nixon's a tough son of a bitch. I don't pretend it's going to be easy."

"Well, you've got a brain trust here, Jack," he said motioning toward O'Brien and O'Donnell. "And I'm just a first term congressman from Bayonne, but the hurdles are already setting up."

"Hurdles? Oh, yes, we've got hurdles," Kennedy joked. "Youth, inexperience, soft on Communism and Catholic to boot. That about it, Neil?"

"Since you bring it up," said O'Donnell before Gallagher could answer. "We all like a good fight. What are your thoughts?"

"Hit them head on. It's the only way," Gallagher insisted, not knowing where O'Donnell was coming from, but seizing the opportunity to tell Kennedy what he genuinely felt. "Do a Nixon-on-Nixon. Position the question in its most favorable light, then answer it before he does it for you."

Gallagher wasn't sure about O'Donnell or O'Brien, but Kennedy seemed interested. "For example?"

"Youth? Turn it into an advantage. With *Sputnik* up there circling the globe, does anyone believe that Eisenhower or Nixon has kept pace? Soft on Communism? You're a war hero, Jack. You fought while Nixon could only talk with Hiss and all the rest about it. Catholic? Concede publicly that it's a problem for some and appeal to Americans' basic sense of fairness. No one wants to be a bigot. Explain how you would separate affairs of state from religion in a speech. Most people see themselves as fair. Position this Catholic thing as an opportunity for them to prove it."

Kennedy nodded. "Not bad. There's a difference of opinion on how to handle some of these issues." He glanced at O'Donnell. "But those are some goddamned good ideas." He walked toward him, extending his hand. "The Kennedy administration is going to be talking about a New Frontier: space, civil rights, economic expansion and an end to this arms race with the Soviets that threatens to destroy our very existence. Peace, Prosperity, Progress. In the end, that's what it's all about, isn't it?"

Gallagher stood and shook his hand. "Yeah, Jack. Those are the ideas we believe in."

The comment was genuine. Gallagher believed in Kennedy and the ideals he tried to turn into reality in America. But as events stood, even then, there were massive challenges confronting the Kennedy campaign. As early as December, 1958, the candidate had gathered a brain trust second to none, consisting of liberal intellectuals from Harvard and MIT like Archibald Cox, Arthur Schlesinger Jr., John Kenneth Galbraith and others. Still, it would take more than an advisory committee and hard campaigning to win his party's nomination or the presidency.

Overall, Kennedy's stints in the House and Senate had been less than stellar. To many, he was immature; more of father Joe's creation than an authentic leader, and best remembered for his absences rather than attendance in Congress and a penchant for autographing 8x10 glossies of himself during tedious sessions. More to the point, Kennedy, despite his youth, carried as much baggage into his campaign as strength. When he visited Eleanor Roosevelt, trying to win her support in early 1960, she refused, berating him for his and Bobby's failure to disavow McCarthy during his Senate hearings and absenting himself from the vote on his censure two years earlier. Former president Harry Truman, too, refused to endorse him, wary of his inexperience and of the risk of having a Roman Catholic on the ticket.[1]

Then, there was the double-edged sword personified in Joe Kennedy. As much despised for his ruthless business practices as he was feared politically for his rumored ties with organized crime, he allegedly helped finance and pull the strings behind his son's presidential bid calling in IOUs from all around the country on his behalf. Cardinal Richard Cushing of Boston later said, "I'll tell you who elected Jack Kennedy. It was his father, Joe, and me, right here in this room." Referring to the West Virginia primary, he went on to explain how he had decided which Protestant ministers should receive "contributions" of $100 to $500 in order to secure their support. "It's good for the Lord. It's good for the church. It's good for the preacher and it's good for the candidate."[2]

Cardinal Cushing wasn't alone in his good works on behalf of the young Kennedy, and before the campaign was over, Frank Sinatra along with people like Sam Giancana, Johnny Roselli and others would make similar claims.

Giancana and Roselli, Joe's sometime golfing buddies, would later be overheard on FBI wiretaps discussing the donations they'd made during the vital West Virginia primary. Of course, J. Edgar Hoover knew all about these ties.[3]

A mass of information suggests that Mafia money and influence were solicited and received to ensure Jack's nomination and election, including an account by Bill Bonanno, son of Joseph "Joe Bananas" Bonanno, godfather of New York's Bonanno crime family. According to Bill, Joe Kennedy tried on several occasions to convince his father to support and help fund Jack's election. But there were deep divisions among the Mafia bosses. Santo Trafficante of Tampa, Florida, and Carlos Marcello of New Orleans, for example, saw Lyndon Johnson as more calculable because of his ties to prominent businessmen with money for extreme right-wing organizations.

Finally, during a particularly stormy gathering held at the Los Angeles Hilton, Tommy Luchese of New York, received a call directly from Joe Kennedy trying to gain a unified commitment. After a strenuous argument, both Trafficante and Marcello agreed that if Joe Kennedy could assure them that Lyndon Johnson would be named vice president on a Kennedy ticket, they could, as a group, get behind his son.[4]

Of course, there were many rumors concerning the way Johnson was chosen, but Bill Bonanno recounted the events leading up to the convention as witness to the Mafia's probable influence:

> So the next day, a day before the balloting began, Luchese and I drove out to actress Marion Davies' estate in Beverly Hills.... We found Joe Kennedy sitting by the swimming pool, all by himself. He was waiting for us . . . when we sat down, Tommy Luchese put our proposal to him.
>
> "I think we're in great shape if you go along," he said. "But we need to know what you think. We think Lyndon Johnson would be an ideal running mate for Jack."
>
> There was the briefest pause. Whatever he was feeling,

Kennedy's expression did not change.

"I think it's a terrific idea, Tommy," he said. That was it. He stood up, extended his hand and smiled. The deal was done.[5]

All of these events were, of course, a long way from Gallagher, who in many ways had more in common with the Kennedy image than the candidate himself. From a local point of view he was going into the April primaries with a strong hand of cards, earned through hard work and caring about his constituents. State Senator Jim Murray, who he'd beaten two years earlier, was hesitant to take him on again, which left Gallagher virtually unopposed.

What's more, however one viewed it, he'd been an effective spokesman and legislator for the 13th District. In addition to his early work on the privacy issue, he'd already earned a reputation as a vocal liberal. He'd prepared a study of the European Common Market adopted by the State Department along with Congressman Frank Coffin, Democrat from Maine; authored an amendment that would withhold aid to the United Arab Republic for the boycott of Israel; sponsored Kennedy's minimum wage bill; and piloted a medical aid bill for the elderly through a new Social Security plan. As important, during these glacial days of the Cold War, he'd been a staunch supporter of a strong defense and an implacable opponent of Communism and its spread through Cuba and into Latin America, Africa and Asia.

Overall, Gallagher found himself closely allied with Kennedy on most major issues, but nowhere was their relationship more profound than on the cause of civil rights. His commitment was demonstrated long before it was fashionable in an appeal to Secretary of State Christian Herter for a United Nations investigation into desecrations of Jewish synagogues in West Germany and in an unyielding determination to secure voting rights for African Americans in the South through the passage of the 1960 Voting Rights Act. When the bill seemed destined to fail, it was Gallagher who led 175 members of the House in launching a petition urging its release from the Rules Committee where it had been stalled for months. In what was to be a precursor to President Kennedy's landmark television appeal to the nation on the subject, he took the floor of the House "to renew a previous suggestion that President Eisenhower make a special radio/TV address to the nation on civil rights. It is important that presidential and moral leadership be expressed on an issue which is essentially a basic human right guaranteed by the Constitution."

Nowhere in his career, however, was Gallagher's commitment to individual rights more strenuously tested than in the bone-chilling nightmare experienced by a twenty-four-year-old African American resident of Bayonne named James "Jimmy" Fair.

# THE PRIVACY WAR

# VII
# Jimmy Fair and Due Process

**"The man was tried, convicted and sentenced to the electric chair, all within forty-eight hours."**

On May 26, 1960, while on his way to visit Rick in the hospital after she had given birth to their third daughter, Patrice, Gallagher received a call from Gene Farrell, editor of the *Jersey Journal*. An African-American man named Jimmy Fair had passed through Blakely, a rural Georgia town, he explained. Hours later, the lifeless body of eight-year-old Yvonne Holmes was discovered in the woods less than a mile from town, beaten and raped. Fair, the main suspect, was arrested, tried, convicted and sentenced to the electric chair, all within forty-eight hours.

Gallagher went to the hospital to visit Rick and his new daughter. He stood holding Patrice with six-year-old Chrissy clinging to his leg, knowing that in three hours he'd be headed for Newark Airport to board a plane to Atlanta. Rick understood that he had to leave. She understood not only the circumstances, but also the unspoken honor code of elected officials at that time in Hudson County, which the community worked and lived by each day.

Prior discussions requesting a stay of execution proved futile as the state of Georgia insisted that Fair had received due process. Still, Gallagher knew under normal circumstances, trials for a capital offense take a minimum of five months. It was clear to him that this had nothing to do with guilt or innocence. Gallagher was not about to watch a modern-day lynching.

On his way to the airport, thinking about the Fair incident, Gallagher thought of the Sacco and Vanzetti trial. The trial of Nicola Sacco and Bartolomeo Vanzetti, who were falsely accused of murdering a guard and paymaster of a shoe factory in Braintree, Massachusetts, quickly became an international spectacle. But Gallagher couldn't help imagine the concern it must have generated in cities made up largely of immigrants not so unlike them. Were they guilty? Would they receive a fair trial? Judge Webster Thayer made up his mind early on, identifying them with racial slurs.

When the verdict was read, few were surprised. Still, the two proclaimed their innocence and for six years fought to have their case reopened. But even after a convicted killer confessed to the crime, authorities held fast, and on August 23, 1927, the two men were executed.

Only a little earlier, with revolutions erupting overseas, Stalin taking over the leadership of Russia, and the founding of the Communist Party in China, rumblings about a "red menace" were heard. The fear of communism, socialism and anarchy were real, so much so that Congress enacted its first quota bill, the National Origins Act of 1924.

The act discriminated against Italians, Poles and Jews, among other groups to curtail immigration from southern and eastern Europe, whose peoples were considered a dual threat to the American political system and to the job security of American workers. The net effect of all of these influences helped to make Hudson County a unique, localized culture that vaunted patriotism, encouraged straightforward honesty and viewed politicians as family members who could be depended on to award jobs and distribute favors in return for loyalty and votes.

Gallagher remembers hearing stories about John Kenny standing on a street corner jingling coins in his pocket and waiting for his favor-seeking neighbors to approach. "Johnny, the wife is sick," one would say. "Johnny, I've been laid off." "Johnny, the cops picked up my kid last night." This was the basis of the system, the "machine" as it came to be known.

When Gallagher arrived in Atlanta, it was apparent that the Georgia justice system was not about to budge.

"Okay," Gallagher said. "Time to play hardball. I'll call a press conference right now to let the world know what justice is like for Blacks in the State of Georgia."

Gallagher's pleas worked. That evening, Fair was granted a 60-day stay of execution while the facts of the case were evaluated. Yet, subsequent appeals for a new trial were denied, and with time and money running out, Fair's attorney, Ray Brown, retained the services of a former soldier-of-fortune turned private investigator now working out of Jersey City: Lou Raino. What lawyers and politicians couldn't do, Brown figured, Raino could, which was to investigate the crime scene and locate witnesses from the posse that initially found the girl. On August 23, Fair's execution was resentenced for September 2 as a result of a confession that he reportedly gave. The confession however, Gallagher argued, was taken by force.

Four days later, at a mass rally held at Salem Baptist Church, Gloster B. Current, national director of the National Association for the Advancement of Colored People (NAACP), gave an impassioned speech expressing grave doubt that Fair had received anything close to a fair trial. Similar sentiments were echoed by Samuel Williams, president of the New Jersey chapter of the

NAACP. Fair had hundreds of supporters, and more than $5,000 was raised to help finance a last-ditch effort to revoke his execution based on a writ of habeas corpus to the Georgia Supreme Court. Then a bombshell was dropped—Ray Brown uncovered indisputable evidence that Fair's confession was taken by force.

After all the legal wrangling, Fair was released from prison on July 20, 1962. A public thank-you from Fair and his parents was given at a political dinner held for Gallagher on October 14, 1962, a night Gallagher would never forget because on that night, according to later allegations by *Life* magazine, Gallagher disposed from his basement the corpse of a man named Barney O'Brien.[1]

# VIII
# The Election of JFK

**"It's Hoover. Neil, you have no idea what this guy and Nixon are doing to family supporters and me."**

The Democratic primaries leading to the presidential convention in Los Angeles were a walk-through for Gallagher that year. Having made a name for himself both locally and in Washington through his work on the Foreign Affairs Committee, key political figures such as Kennedy and House majority leader John McCormack offered unwavering support for his renomination, calling Gallagher the most outstanding young congressman he had ever encountered in Washington.

The ride into the November general election seemed only slightly more difficult, his opponent being Samuel Kanis, the Jersey City attorney he'd soundly trounced two years earlier by a three to one margin.

If the obstacles on the local front for Gallagher were less than onerous, those that still needed to be overcome by Jack Kennedy were steeped in peril. His Roman Catholicism remained an issue, so much so that in the primary of West Virginia, where only 5 percent of the population was Catholic, Hubert Humphrey chose "Give Me That Old Time Religion" as his campaign song.

The coattails of his father, too, were long but infested with a malignancy that no amount of campaign rhetoric could cure. Lyndon Johnson, running number two in the presidential polls at the time, was savage in his loathing of the senator, attempting whenever possible to tie the elder Kennedy's past to the candidate. And even as Kennedy took on all comers in seven consecutive primaries in states not overly friendly to New England Harvardites, such as Oregon, Wisconsin, Nebraska and West Virginia, former party standard-bearer Harry Truman resigned as a delegate not wanting to be party to a pre-arranged affair. In speaking of "John," he pretended a slip, calling him "Joe," and when questioned about Kennedy's Roman Catholicism, he scratched his head wondering whether he should be more concerned about the "Pop" or the "Pope."[1]

The visible terrain going into the convention in Los Angeles was not too pretty, but Gallagher recognized something else going on as America embarked on this new decade: History had begun to favor Kennedy. Nineteen sixty was the year the U.S. Food and Drug Administration (FDA) approved the world's first oral contraceptive, a tiny white tablet that hit the nation with the social ferocity of the atom bomb. In Greensboro, four African-American freshmen from North Carolina A&T sat down in protest at an all-white lunch counter in Woolworth's department store. Joined by 85 additional activists, the sit-in sparked non-violent demonstrations across the country opening a new phase of the civil rights movement.

In music, it was Chubby Checker and the Twist, an apt metaphor for the coming sexual revolution, and in world affairs it was the catastrophic U-2 incident where CIA pilot Francis Gary Powers' U-2 spy plane was shot down above the USSR. The Eisenhower administration claimed it was a civilian craft that had somehow drifted into Soviet air space. Unfortunately, it was Khrushchev who held the trump card since Powers survived the crash, had been captured and already confessed to high-altitude spying.

With all that was going on, American politics needed a bridge, someone to fill the gap between Eisenhower, rooted deep in the traditions of the World War II power structure and someone younger, more vigorous, even sexy, who would lead America into the modern space age where competition was keen and minds sharp. The landscape was, indeed, a new frontier.

The 1960 Democratic National Convention opened on July 11 in the new Los Angeles Sports Arena. Just days before, a congressional quarterly poll of senators and representatives showed that 54 percent of the members responding thought Johnson was the party's strongest candidate, while only 20 percent named Kennedy. Former president Harry Truman, determined to sit out the convention, publicly endorsed Stuart Symington of Missouri. But these were the opinions of the insiders, the party bosses, not the delegates or masses that voted. And the people loved JFK.

He spent this time traveling on his private plane *Caroline* zigzagging across the country more than a dozen times since 1957. He attended meetings held in schools and churches, campaigned in primaries, appeared regularly on television shows such as *Meet the Press* and *Face the Nation* and capitalized on his father's wealth and war heroics. All of these efforts, put forward by a team of Madison Avenue PR wizards, had created something much bigger than a man. An image had been created, and party insiders had never before seen anything quite like it.

Even the ultimate political carnivore, Lyndon Johnson, who just six days earlier had formally entered the race, could not calculate the depth of the Kennedy sweep. "He's winning those beauty contests," he told aide Bobby Baker. "But when it gets down to the nut-cutting he won't have the bulls with him."[2] But Johnson was wrong, and even as the gathering convened early that evening, the Kennedy nomination seemed sure, which was all the more frustrating for Gallagher and other ardent Kennedy backers trapped in the middle of New Jersey governor Meyner's obsession with being the state's "favorite son."

The Meyner-Kennedy relationship played a significant role at the convention as far as the New Jersey delegation was concerned. In some ways, it was humorous. They just did not like each other. On the Easter holiday preceding the convention, Gallagher and Rick, along with Meyner and his wife, Helen, were guests of Bob and Gloria Conahay at the Buccaneer Lodge in Marathon, Florida. Gallagher and Meyner would play tennis during the day but at dinner they would argue about Jack Kennedy.

The governor was adamant in his estimation that Kennedy was nothing but a "rich phony," referring to Jackie Kennedy's pregnancy as a "political pregnancy" that would be non-existent when the convention was over. On the other hand, Kennedy's sense of humor barely overshadowed his disdain for Meyner. Periodically, Gallagher would have lunch in the senator's office, and they would discuss the makeup of the potential delegation from New Jersey. Kennedy would have a checklist and they would go over who might be supportive and who might not.

Most of the time, since Gallagher was from New Jersey, Kennedy would question him about certain individuals. But when it came to Meyner, he said, "Let me size him up first, see if I'm right. Up until now, he was the bright young man of the party and he resents that I'm younger. Next, he's an ex-Catholic and they're the worst when it comes to the idea of a Catholic president. But Neil, this is the main reason he will never vote for me and I'll never get his support: I take a better picture than the son of a bitch, and

he'll never forgive me for that." Kennedy then broke out laughing
and so did Gallagher, but in the end, as things turned out, it was a
fair assessment.

The night before they balloted, there was a meeting of the
New Jersey delegation. The Kennedy supporters had about thirty
votes out of the state's forty-one. John Kenny, Dave Wilintz,
Denny Carey, Thorn Lord and George Brunner were the political
leaders who made up the state's party. Gallagher was the Kennedy
liaison. The meeting became acrimonious. Prior to it, Gallagher
had visited Jack and Bobby's room where Sergeant Shriver and
Kenny O'Donnell were planning Jack's run. Bobby showed
Gallagher their tally that indicated they had the votes for a win on
the first ballot, though it was understood nothing was for certain.

Gallagher reported this back to the New Jersey delegates.
Meyner stood up and argued there was no way they had enough
votes, insisting that his name be placed in nomination for the "pres-
tige of the state." Actually, the anti-Kennedy group was hoping to
stop a first-ballot nomination. A lot of arguments took place, going
on for hours. Finally Kenny, who wasn't feeling well, left the room
saying that Gallagher would speak for him and that any decision
made by Gallagher would have his and the Hudson County delegation's support.

The debate went on until Thorn Lord suggested a one-hour
recess so that Gallagher could check in with the Kennedy group to
see how they wanted to handle the dilemma since it appeared that
Meyner's insistence would split the delegation the next day during
a floor vote. Gallagher went over and explained the New Jersey situation to Bobby and Shriver. They got Jack on the phone. Shriver
then speculated that while they thought they had enough votes to
win on the first ballot, they could lose a few first ballot votes that
had been committed if something unexpected happened. The deci-

sion was that if Gallagher could get Meyner committed to vote for Kennedy on the second roll call, it might be better to keep the delegation together and vote Meyner as "favorite son" on the first roll call with the entire New Jersey delegation agreed to vote for Kennedy on the second in case they fell short.

Gallagher went back once the meeting reconvened and reported the idea. This provided Meyner with his "favorite son" nomination and placated the Kennedy delegates. The governor agreed and that was their position.

The next day, as the voting started, everyone understood that a first ballot nomination would be extremely close. As voting progressed, Gallagher told Meyner that he believed Kennedy had the votes. Meyner insisted that he did not. As the roll call progressed, television cameras and radio broadcasters gathered in front of the New Jersey delegation. If the delegation went for Kennedy it would clinch the nomination for him and Meyner would appear to be the king maker and hero of the convention.

"It's over, Jack's got it," Gallagher urged. "For god's sake vote the delegation for Kennedy."

But with all of the media glaring at him in anticipation, Meyner simply froze. "They don't have it. They don't have it," he kept repeating, but by the time the voting got to Wyoming, it was all over. Kennedy had won on the first ballot. The convention went wild and a motion was made to nominate by acclamation. There was no need for a second roll call. Meyner slumped into his chair. In the end, Jack Kennedy had been right months earlier when he said, "There are three reason Bob Meyner will never support me."

Kennedy and Gallagher would confer often between the convention and the November election with Gallagher crafting his own campaign around issues they shared including defense, the space program, the need for an A-bomb test ban treaty and civil rights. During that time, Kennedy held campaign rallies in Hudson County twice, one in mid-September, then again in Jersey City's Journal Square on Sunday, November 6, just two days before the general election.

On a wooden platform set in the north corner of the square with 100,000 screaming supporters stood John Kennedy at a podium flanked by Gallagher, John Kenny, Governor Meyner and Congressman Dominick Daniels. The atmosphere was rip-roaring contagious and "Kennedy for President, Gallagher for Congress" signs were posted everywhere. Adoring women and cheering men held up homemade, "I'd Give the Shirt Off My Back for Jack" and "Welcome, Mr. President" placards.

Just before he began to speak, as the mayor was introducing him, he turned to Gallagher, pointing to a lone "Gallagher's Our Man" banner hung from the very pinnacle of the lofty Lowe's clock tower.

"Say, Neil, who's running for president here anyway? Is it me or you?"

"It's you, of course, Mr. President," he answered.

"Good. Just thought I'd ask." Kennedy grinned before stepping up to the podium to address the throng of supporters with the message he'd been driving home for more than two years; his own ideas about the future, still shrouded by the ghost of Joe McCarthy and the pall of Cold War anti-Communism.

"Four years ago the Cold War was being carried on thousands of miles away," Kennedy's voice rang out over the speaker system. "This year it spread to within 90 miles of Florida, to Cuba. Next week when Mr. Khrushchev and Mr. Castro arrive in New York, they will bring the Cold War within 12 miles of Journal Square. And yet the administration has told us that all is well. In the 1930s while England slept, Hitler armed. Today, while we stand still,

Khrushchev moves, and, I tell you, we must rebuild our nation's defenses because it is not a question of quarreling with Mr. Khrushchev, as Mr. Nixon has done. It is a question of making ourselves stronger than Russia. Talk is cheap. But now we must help the rising peoples in the underdeveloped regions of the world to find their way to self-government and seize the initiative in this Cold War with bold imaginative programs launched with good will and launched from strength."

The speech was greeted with near-hysterical approval and it took Kennedy a full fifteen minutes to get off the platform despite a heavy cordon of police. He shook hands with everyone he could reach as he moved slowly toward the waiting motorcade. Many women in the crowd tried to kiss him, while others could be seen crying. "God bless you, Johnny," many shouted.

When he got to his open car, along with Gallagher and Meyner, who rode with him, thousands lined the streets, shouting, waving flags or just staring as the caravan of a half dozen Cadillac's and Lincoln's headed toward Newark Airport.

Once they'd arrived at the airport, Gallagher was walking alone with Kennedy on the tarmac toward the *Caroline* when they shared a strange and harrowing moment. They approached the foot of the stairs leading to the plane and were about to say good-bye, but Kennedy had fallen silent. His upbeat demeanor disappeared as if someone had pulled a plug. "Jesus, Jack, what's wrong?"

Kennedy shook his head, worried and depressed. "It's Hoover. Neil, you have no idea what this guy and Nixon are doing to me. Investigations by the FBI. Audits by the IRS. The bastard's got us all under constant surveillance and it scares the shit out of me."

Gallagher put his arm around him. "Jack, don't worry. By Tuesday, you'll be commander in chief of this nation. Then, Hoover and Nixon and all of this will be forgotten. Incidentally, this is probably the last time I can call you Jack, Mr. President."

Kennedy smiled a little. "I sure as hell hope you're right." He climbed the stairs into the plane.

Four days later, Gallagher was elected to his second term in Congress by the widest margin of victory in any of the New Jersey races and John Kennedy became the thirty-fifth president of the United States, having won the election over Richard Nixon by just 112,803 votes, one of the slimmest margins in American history.

## IX
## The New President

**"Gallagher realized this wasn't the same John Kennedy of even three months before."**

Immediately following the victory it seemed only natural that stories of irregular practices would swirl through the press and political circles. It was long rumored that much of Joe Kennedy's fortune was derived from prohibition bootlegging in league with people like Chicago mayor Richard Daly and Mob boss Frank Costello. Beyond that, anyone close to John Kennedy was aware of his fascination with Frank Sinatra and his pals, many of whom were associated with organized crime. Then there was Jack's problem with women. His ever-loyal secretary Evelyn Lincoln would later remark "He never chased women; they chased him."[1] Nevertheless, his affairs with Angie Dickinson, Marilyn Monroe and Judith Campbell, Sam Giancana's off-and-on-again mistress, did not escape J. Edgar Hoover's eye.

Campbell revealed in an interview shortly before her death that Jack called her one afternoon and told her to go to her mother's house and call from there. When she did, he said that Hoover was tapping the phone in her apartment. Hoover, he said, clearly knew about their relationship, that she'd been to the White House and that they both had ties to organized crime. Campbell believed that Hoover, knowing that Jack wanted him out of office, was ensuring his job by letting Kennedy know who was boss.[2] Shortly after on November 10, 1960, at his first formal news conference, Kennedy announced the reappointment of Hoover as FBI director and Allen Dulles as head of the CIA.

This was nothing new. Hoover had been blackmailing presidents since the 1930s. He was not a man anyone wanted to fool with and, at that time, with the Cold War revved to a fevered pitch, he was at the height of his power. According to Gallagher, it was no coincidence that Hoover came out on top. Congress, the other agencies, even the Executive Branch, lived in fear of him.

Nevertheless, Kennedy eventually did take on Allen Dulles after the Bay of Pigs. The CIA had briefed him at this retreat in Palm Beach as early as November 18, 1960. At that time, mindful of the fact that Cuba had already established military ties to the Soviet Union, Kennedy was reluctant, but agreed to go along provided that the U.S. military would not become directly involved, which, he believed, would start a nuclear war with the Soviets.

Shortly after the election, Gallagher met with Kennedy in the Oval Office to discuss the closing of Caven Point Army Base, but the subject quickly turned to Cuba as the president, who'd just wrapped up a meeting with Secretary of State Dean Rusk, walked around his desk to sit in a chair directly across from him.

"Two years ago," Gallagher began, "I met with Secretary of State Herter and Dick Bissell with what I thought was compelling evidence that Russian technicians were setting up missile sites and training Cuban soldiers to use them. Mr. President, those missiles were pointed at the United States. No one was interested. Frankly, I couldn't believe it."

"Herter is gone," said Kennedy sitting back in his chair, lighting a cigar.

"And the missiles I spoke with Herter about, Mr. President? Are they gone?" The president just sat surrounded by a cloud of smoke.

It was then that Gallagher realized this wasn't the same John Kennedy of even three months before. He'd always seen Jack as a man of many dimensions, happy-go-lucky, charming, witty and genuinely funny. But now he looked tense and uneasy. His legendary sense of humor deserted him. He fidgeted with his cigar and explained that any overt action would be suicide, that it would be viewed as first strike against Khrushchev.

"If we had understood Castro's ties to the Soviet Union when he first came into power," Gallagher asserted, "he wouldn't have risen to the position he enjoys today. With all due respect, Mr. President, I lay that at the doorstep of the CIA."

Kennedy contemplated Gallagher's argument. "What are you suggesting, Neil?"

"As I understand it, the worst-kept secret in the country right now has to do with thousands of Cuban exiles being trained by the United States in the Florida Everglades to return to Cuba," Gallagher argued. "The American people need to be informed. I'd verify that there are missiles or troops down there. That's the real issue. If the threat is genuine, Mr. President, hold the Soviet Union accountable to world opinion now before it's too late."

Kennedy slowly put out his cigar. "Thanks, Neil," he said, and then stood to leave. "I'll take your thoughts into consideration."

Gallagher could see that the president was both confused and distracted. If only he'd been briefed on the matter, Gallagher says today. But Kennedy, driven by the momentum of pre-election rhetoric and former President Eisenhower's approval of the plan, felt compelled to do something.

The new president undoubtedly depended on the advice of others, some from the intelligence community like Dulles and Bissell, others from the State Department like Chester Bowles and Dean Rusk. Still, with attempts at assassination failing and Soviet weapons pouring into Cuba on a daily basis, the odds of success were never very high. It was here that Kennedy's inexperience surfaced in ways both subtle and obvious.

On the afternoon of April 18, 1961, thirty-six hours after the invasion had begun, not a single element of the Bay of Pigs had succeeded. Castro was still alive. One CIA-sponsored air attack emanating from Nicaragua had minimal results with a second having been canceled. Castro's army, fully prepared for the assault, had killed 114 men and captured another 1,189. Castro's spies among the Cuban exiles in Florida had given him the entire plan, thus bringing about the most significant international embarrassment of the Kennedy administration.

In a televised address to the American public, the president denied direct U.S. involvement in the attack, but in an oblique reference to indirect involvement noted, "There is an old saying that victory has 100 fathers and defeat is an orphan." The subtlety of the comment was not lost on political analysts or Republican adversaries who viewed the entire affair as a major embarrassment to the United States before the world community. A shocked and irate Kennedy immediately demanded a thorough analysis of the debacle and as a first move recalled General Maxwell Taylor from civilian life to recast the country's paramilitary planning including "intelligence, guerrilla activity and any other pursuit to gain politico-military objectives."[3]

On May 23, 1961, Allen Dulles appeared before the House Foreign Affairs Committee where Gallagher, furious at what happened and what he knew about the Bay of Pigs, aggressively cross-examined him. The issue of air support had already become controversial when Dulles publicly asserted it had been pledged, then withdrawn, forcing Kennedy to refute the director's allegation in a speech given that same month at American University. Since the Foreign Affairs Committee sessions were closed, few would hear the postmortem, but today Gallagher can be more candid about the real story behind the Bay of Pigs and what happened at those hearings.

Unbelievably, Dulles put forward the view that the invasion missed "by a hair's breadth"[4] and though only 1,400 rebels were involved, in his mind, it was not a failure because the invader established a beachhead regardless of the fact that it couldn't be maintained against Castro's tanks and fighter planes. The implication was that if they'd had air support to knock those tanks and planes out, they would have made it.

While this may or may not be true, the fact of the matter was that Kennedy had made it crystal clear that direct involvement of U.S. military personnel, ground or air, was out of the question. As it turned out, Dulles had betrayed him, knowing it was necessary, but believing that once things got underway and the need for air support was obvious, he could coerce the president into capitulating.

In the end, he just didn't know Kennedy, was not truthful with him and abysmally misread the situation, which to Gallagher was the ultimate intelligence disaster. But Dulles was implacable. He knew that the president would not commit the United States Air Force but never admitted the mistake and, in fact, tried publicly to humiliate him over it.

Just three months later, Allen Dulles, an intelligence community icon for nearly thirty years, was unceremoniously fired from his position as director of the CIA by Kennedy. Gallagher believes it was an indignity that would cause the aging spymaster/assassin to quietly hate the new president for the rest of his life.

# THE PRIVACY WAR

# X
# Privacy in the Church

**"...demanded that she have sex with him, threatening to send a recording of her confession to her husband."**

Gallagher's relationship with Roy Cohn during these tumultuous times with Cuba and Berlin dwindled to chance encounters at the 21 Club, the Cub Room of the Stork Club or at one of Cohn's famous parties held at the Park Avenue apartment he shared with his mother, Dora. Still, Cohn's invaluable contacts, such as New York's Cardinal Francis Spellman, came in handy for the congressman.

Cohn was great friends with the cardinal. Through him he met with people such as Walter Winchell and Joe McCarthy regularly. Later, with Winchell not the factor that he used to be and McCarthy having drunk himself to death in 1957, the cardinal's relationship with Cohn flourished.

So it was that Cohn told Gallagher one day in early 1961 that Spellman wanted to meet him at his residency for lunch. When Gallagher arrived at the Cardinal's residence behind Saint Patrick's Cathedral in New York City, there were dozens of police, FBI and firemen blocking off the street and sidewalk. The rectory was tied in yellow police ribbon. The cardinal explained that a bomb had gone off in front of the rectory that very morning. In his semi-Irish, pious manner, he expressed his concern about how terrible it was and how thankful he was that no one had been injured. After some time, to break the ice, Gallagher, with a deadpan expression, asked Spellman if he believed that either Eleanor Roosevelt or Cardinal Cushing were responsible for the explosion, as both were not great admirers of his Eminence. The Cardinal ignored the remark and Cohn kicked him under the table. "His Eminence did not think that was funny!"

Of course, quips Gallagher now, "Both Roy and the cardinal were very serious commie fighters."

After lunch the cardinal invited Gallagher to speak with him privately. They went into a side room. Spellman said he understood that Gallagher was very friendly with President Kennedy. He then confided that his only hobby and vice in his life was his stamp collection and that he had been receiving first issue stamps since the Coolidge administration. However, he pointed out, through some omission he was not receiving first issue stamps under the Kennedy administration. He asked if Gallagher could remind the president to put him back on the first issue stamp collection list.

The next week Gallagher was in the White House to meet the president. When he found the occasion, Gallagher told him he'd had lunch with the cardinal who asked him to deliver a message. "For Christ's sake," Kennedy said before he could deliver another word. "He's not asking about those stamps again." Gallagher broke out laughing. "The next time you see that old son of a bitch tell him to get his stamps from the man he voted for: Dick Nixon."

Several months later, in May 1961, Gallagher took advantage of Cohn's introduction and went to see Cardinal Spellman without an appointment. Thousands of letters were now pouring into Gallagher's office as a result of widespread government abuses that his Privacy Committee was uncovering and which were widely reported by the media and editorial comment around the country. Some were shocking and some were sickening. One letter from a woman in Morristown, New Jersey was so compelling that he went to Spellman with it.

The letter was written by a Catholic woman who regularly attended confession and communion. One afternoon, after leaving the church and going to confession, a man approached her on the stairs and demanded that she have sex with him, threatening to send a recording of her confession to her husband. He then proceeded to play back the incriminating recording which he'd made using a parabolic microphone. Neither was she the first, nor would she be the last, he claimed, as it was his practice to record the confessions of attractive women and then use the tapes to make his advances.

The letter, which had been authenticated by Gallagher's office, was especially appalling to him, he told Spellman, since he had daughters himself who attended Catholic schools and went to confession and communion on a regular basis. "This," Gallagher said, "is a classic privacy issue that could destroy people, families and subject anyone to blackmail. Actions like this pervert the fundamental tenets of the Catholic faith and undermine the concept of redemption that is the basis of forgiveness and renewal of a troubled person by the absolution of God."

"My son, don't worry about things like this," the cardinal replied. "Mr. Hoover protects us from all of these unpleasantries."

Gallagher, needless to say, was shocked. "But, your Eminence, these are sacraments. How do we know how widespread something like this might be? This type of equipment, parabolic microphones and such, are used almost exclusively by security people and the FBI. How can we know who did this, if we don't investigate. What are you and the Church going to do to protect your people, or are the Sacraments now inoperative because no one wants to know what's really happening in the outside world and the effect technology is having on people?"

"This is not your concern, my son," the cardinal repeated. Gallagher finally gave up. Cardinal Spellman, he concluded, simply did not care.

Several months later while dining at the Stork Club, Cohn offered Gallagher a briefcase filled with hundreds of dossiers assembled by the HUAC on suspected homosexuals working at the State Department.

"While no one's suggesting that a man or woman's homosexuality makes them a Communist," Cohn explained, "I believe it fair to say that their homosexuality makes them an easy target for Communists. We feel that you and the Foreign Affairs Committee need to take up the baton on this. You could be big with this, Neil. Fighting the Communist threat here at home can make a hero of a man like you. You could be the new Joe McCarthy."

Gallagher gave him a hard stare. "Are you nuts?" he cried. "Why the hell would I want to be the new Joe McCarthy? I despised the old Joe McCarthy."

Gallagher would not see Cohn for many months following, partly owing to schedules, mostly due to design. Their paths though would eventually cross again, however, this time with disastrous consequences.

# XI
# Personality Testing

**"She was fired because she refused to relinquish her
Fourth Amendment right."**

Going into 1962, Gallagher focused mostly on nuclear disarmament, meaningful civil rights legislation, measures to stem the rising tide of narcotics and local drug rehabilitation programs. The
issue of governmental intrusions into the private lives of civilians,
however, would not go away. A new world of information opened
up to him when he learned of personality testing.

The personality testing was developed as part of Operation
MKULTRA, a top-secret project begun in 1953. MKULTRA had its
roots in another Special Operations project known as BLUE-
BEARD, whose primary objective was to learn how to covertly
modify an individual's behavior. The year BLUEBEARD was first set
in motion, 1952, was also the year that the Chinese government,
during the Korean War, launched a propaganda campaign featuring
filmed confessions of captured U.S. pilots, expressionless and
robotic, as they admitted to the use of germ warfare, among other
war crimes. It was around this time that the *Miami News* first published an article titled "Brain-Washing Tactics Force Chinese into
Ranks of Communist Party."This was the first time the word "brain-
washing" or hsi nao, to "cleanse the mind," was ever used in print.[1]

Whereas MKULTRA was used to develop, through drugs and behavioral conditioning, a soldier who would robotically act on command, the personality test was used to control enemies. It was called the "pick the scabs" approach. Once the test had identified a target as having potential weaknesses, members of the team would suggest ways to break him down, such as attempting to destroy his marriage. Next, they might start a rumor campaign against him and harass him constantly.[2]

Though this may have seemed like standard warfare against enemies, these techniques, Gallagher later learned, would eventually be used by the CIA and the FBI under Hoover against U.S. citizens. Among the victims were some of Gallagher's closest friends, including Congressman Hale Boggs, Bobby Kennedy, Jim Garrison, Martin Luther King and, shortly thereafter, Gallagher himself.

One case was that of sixteen-year employee of the U.S. State Department, Mary Gunda-Mullenhof. Gunda-Mullenhof had top-secret security clearance for twelve of her sixteen years in the department and had worked as the personal secretary to four ambassadors in highly sensitive areas around the world. Every three years State Department employees were reevaluated, but this time psychological testing was used. And the questions, according to Gallagher, seemed to focus mostly on sexual and religious topics: Do you believe in God? How often do you go to church? Do you sleep with your mother?

Gunda-Mullenhof was a devout Catholic, was single and had a very close relationship with her widowed mother. She refused to answer the questions, which led the department to label her a security risk. Needless to say, she was not reassigned. In effect, she was fired because she refused to relinquish her Fourth Amendment right to freedom from unnecessary search and seizure.

As a result, Gunda-Mullenhof wrote to Gallagher about the incident and they arranged a meeting. She said she wasn't complaining and understood that she brought this on herself by refusing to answer the questions, but wondered if she might keep, at least, a non-sensitive position—her mother was ill and she needed the money.

Gallagher asked that her record be looked into and if it was as flawless as it seemed, why not overlook the test? After all, not everybody enjoys answering questions about their sexual habits and religious beliefs, he argued, and perhaps she was right in not answering them to begin with.

About a week later, Gallagher got a response refusing his requests, arguing that because Gunda-Mullenhof refused to answer the questions, she obviously had something to hide. This infuriated Gallagher, and he wrote back, outlining his plan not only to hold public hearings on her case, but also on the legality of the State Department screenings in general. Soon after Gallagher received a call explaining how the incident was a mistake on the part of the State Department.

Gunda-Mullenhof was eventually reassigned to a position in Geneva. But by the conclusion of Gallagher's privacy hearings, incontestable evidence would be gathered that both the CIA and FBI were using psychological profiling as a means not only to screen suspected homosexuals out of government, but to create files, which could later be used for blackmail.

In his 1969 book, *The Death Of Privacy*, Jerry Rosenberg warned that legitimate agencies could pay government employees for information just as easily as the Mafia could, which could be used for blackmail or coercion.[3]

What Rosenberg could not envision was a government that, thirty years later, had pooled its computer resources into a law enforcement network involving the CIA, FBI, IRS and more than sixty other government agencies to systematize their records on U.S. citizens, making every individual a potential target for investigation.

# XII
# JFK and the Cuban Missile Crisis

**"After all, Neil, one Bay of Pigs per lifetime is enough."**

On Tuesday, October 16, 1962, shortly before 9:00 A.M., Kennedy's assistant for National Security Affairs, McGeorge Bundy, brought the president photographs taken from a high-altitude U-2 reconnaissance plane over Cuba showing nuclear-armed IL-28 medium-range missiles targeted on U.S. cities.

If this was the backdrop against which most saw the Cuban missile crisis unfolding, Gallagher had good reason to believe the decision to arm Cuba with nuclear missiles was made long before this, probably sometime in late 1959, as he'd discussed with Bissell three years earlier. Fascinating to Gallagher was that the U.S. intelligence world in its entirety knew nothing about the threat until now. To this day, no one has asked what the preparations were to receive those missiles. The silos were there. They couldn't have been constructed overnight. It took months, perhaps years, of preparation, of design, construction and positioning. Why was this awesome threat totally neglected until the missiles were actually put in place and about to be armed?

In August of that year, the already-volatile situation heated up when the CIA, through its informants, finally began picking up a steady flow of information regarding military equipment arriving at Cuban ports and moving to interior areas under Soviet guard. The issue at hand was the arrival of what was presumed to be surface-to-air missiles and radars. The problem, as CIA director John McCone confided to Kennedy, Rusk and others was that surface-to-air missiles were virtually indistinguishable from medium-range ballistic missiles, which had a range of 350 miles.

Soon after, Republican senator Kenneth Keating of New York, who learned of McCone's findings through a leak, rose to the Senate floor and charged that, due to the Cuban situation, the Halcyon days of John Kennedy were over. Like a clap of thunder, the allegation reverberated around the world as the "Communist threat." All in all, the message was out: Kennedy was "soft on nukes."

Gallagher's last meeting with Kennedy before the Cuban Missile Crisis was on October 12, four days before McCone's discovery. They met in the president's suite at the Hotel Carlyle in New York. Ever-present were three military aides who carried The Football, a black vinyl satchel that contained the codes that the president could use to unleash nuclear war. They later had breakfast along with Kenny O'Donnell and Larry O'Brien, then left Manhattan.

Once on the New Jersey Turnpike, their motorcade was joined by the cars of Newark mayor Hugh Addonizio and New Jersey congressman Pete Rodino. It was then that the conversation turned to election politics and the most obvious issue of Kennedy's presidency: Cuba.

"I've asked McNamara to look into those leaks," Kennedy told Gallagher. "But he's not optimistic. I was hoping to hold some of it back at least until after the election, knowing that if word got out to the press, it would be injected into the campaign. That's exactly what happened."

"We've taken our lumps, Mr. President," Gallagher replied. "But so have you. The question now is, what do we do about it? The last thing anyone needs is for an issue of national security to turn divisive."

"The crime is that Hoover held back information on national security when it first came to your attention in '59," said Kennedy. "It's a crisis now and that's what we're dealing with."

"The horse is out of the barn, Mr. President," O'Donnell injected. "All of this saber rattling is dangerous. We can't let political pressure be the factor that dictates our policy."

The president must have been thinking about *Washington Post* cartoons captions like "Why Johnnie Slept," a reference to his book *Why England Slept*. Other cartoons depicted him during his famous "Ich Bin Ein Berliner" speech in Munich, not Berlin, in a nasty allusion to his father's support of the Munich Accords.

Gallagher knew that Kennedy would respond, and his eyes raised to meet the president's, shocked to notice the deep concern that was etched into his face. It'd been a rough couple of years from the Bay of Pigs, to civil rights, Berlin, Vienna and now this, potentially the single most important moment in the second half of the twentieth century.

Yet Kennedy seemed calm, and it made Gallagher speculate that perhaps the character of all men tends to be shaped by important experiences in their formative years. There was no question that Kennedy had matured since his last brush with Castro. He'd learned the art of objectivity, to live in the calm at the center of the storm.

"In 1914, with World War I underway," Kennedy began, "Prince von Bulow, the former German chancellor said to the current chancellor, Bethmann-Hollweg, 'How did it all happen?' to which Bethmann-Hollweg replied, 'Ah, if only one knew.' If this planet is ever ravaged by nuclear war, if the survivors can endure the fire and radiation and catastrophe, I don't ever want one of those survivors to ask another, 'How did it happen?' and receive the reply 'Ah, if only one knew.' But I'm going to tell you something, that's what Keating and the others are pushing us toward and I don't like it."

"How do you see the situation in Cuba, Mr. President?" Gallagher asked.

"Anatoly Dobrynin spoke with Bobby last week and Adlai only two days ago swearing that Khrushchev has no intention of using Cuba as an offensive military base. Yesterday morning TASS repeated almost the exact words publicly. For now, or at least until we have reason to believe otherwise, I want to keep my options for independent action open." He shot a fleeting smile across the table. "After all, Neil, one Bay of Pigs per lifetime is enough, don't you think?"

Their motorcade met with Rodino and Addonizio's in Newark. From there, the president traveling in a blue Lincoln Continental convertible, with the top down, was driven to Newark City Hall where he addressed a crowd of nearly 150,000. Realizing this was the final destination of the Columbus Day parade and many in attendance were of Italian descent, Kennedy praised the "fine work of my good friend Neil Gallagher," but saved his best remarks for Rodino, the grand marshal, and Addonizio, the newly elected mayor.

"I've never had the courage to make this claim before, but in honor of Congressman Rodino and Mayor Addonizio, I'll make it here on Columbus Day in Newark," he beamed. "My late maternal grandfather, John Fitzgerald, former mayor of Boston, frequently claimed that the Fitzgerald branch of the family was really descended from the Geraldinis, who came from Venice. Now, standing here, seeing you people and thinking of the voyage of Christopher Columbus, probably the outstanding adventure in the annals of human history, I'm starting to be convinced. I believe the

Kennedy's may be part Italian."

The crowd roared its approval. To Gallagher, the oppressive weight of just hours before seemed to have vanished, evaporated like steam into the sunlight, leaving behind this new man brimming with confidence and humor, a prankster, laughing and funny, with not a care in the world.

They left the platform. While walking to the president's car, Kennedy asked Gallagher if he would get him a Coke. Gallagher went to the man running a newsstand, a blind man. "You have a very distinguished customer," he told the man.

"Is it the mayor?"

"No," Gallagher answered. "It's the president of the United States."

The man was shocked. "Could I shake his hand? Could I meet him?"

"Sure," Gallagher said and walked over to tell Kennedy. Kennedy happily came by.

"Could I have a picture taken with you?" the man asked eagerly. The president agreed but all the photographers were still up on the platform. Gallagher then noticed something he would never forget. The president spent more time talking to the blind man alone while waiting for the photographers than he did to his crowd only a few minutes before.

The next morning an article appeared in the *New York Daily Mirror* that outlined a telephone threat to shoot the president, which put police on a special alert in the area of the Lincoln Tunnel Plaza. Deputy Police Commissioner Walter Arm, in charge of community relations, said the caller stated that the president better keep his head down that day, but hung up before the call could be traced.[1] The motorcade passed the area without incident, but in hindsight, the threat was certainly ominous.

The president spent most of the time between October 16 and October 28 of 1962 in the Cabinet Room meeting with ExCom, a committee of national security advisors that included Lyndon Johnson, McNamara, Rusk, Under Secretary George Ball and Bobby Kennedy, among others. Key members of the CIA, Defense and Foreign Affairs Committee were meeting in conference rooms in the White House basement with Kenny O'Donnell running between the groups and the president occasionally breaking to check in on them. From the beginning Kennedy was tense, convinced that Khrushchev was testing his toughness. The question that raged was not whether to act, but how to show resolve without instigating World War III.

By Thursday, October 18, the consensus was for a blockade of Cuba, a limited action that gave the administration time to ponder further strategy. Some argued that if the United States blockaded Cuba, might not the Soviets do the same in Berlin? Further, since Cuba, a sovereign nation, had requested Soviet military assistance, on what legal ground could America stop their ships? The following day, all of these debates ended when new U-2 photographs revealed more medium-range missile sites, along with three intercontinental ballistic missiles vaunting a range of some 2,200 nautical miles.[2]

"The Soviets are building enough launching sites to fire a single volley of missiles capable of killing eighty million Americans," Kennedy confided to O'Donnell after seeing the photos.

There was now tremendous tension. Already, sixty-three ships were in place to enforce a quarantine of the island, but what would happen when a Soviet ship arrived with the remainder of their military hardware? Gallagher recalls Kennedy coming down into the conference room of the White House where he and other members of the Foreign Affairs Committee were meeting.

"How are things in Jersey City? How is Mayor Kenny?" the President asked.

"That depends, Mr. President. Are Jackie and Caroline still upstairs or are they at Camp David?" Gallagher said, knowing that if war were imminent, the First Family would have been evacuated.

"Yes, Neil, they're still upstairs," Kennedy nodded, smiling. "But maybe you guys better work a little harder. There isn't room enough in that hole in Camp David for us all."

By 10:00 A.M. on October 24, McNamara announced that two Russian ships were approaching the quarantine barrier, 500 miles from Cuba. This was the hour when either the Soviets would back down or Kennedy would set in motion the events that could lead to the horrific holocaust all mankind had feared since the coming of the Atomic Age. By 10:25 A.M., word arrived that the Russian ships had stopped dead in the water at the edge of the quarantine line. Khrushchev was clever and what seemed like a stalemate was not. U-2 photos taken that day that showed that the material needed to go on. Missiles were still being assembled. Sites were still being constructed. Understanding that soon all of the missile sites would be ready for activation, the only alternative left to carrying out the president's initiative seemed to be invasion, which would almost certainly escalate into nuclear war.

With U.S. troops on alert in Berlin and the president having decided to begin plans for invasion, John Scali, an ABC-TV State Department correspondent, stepped forward claiming Aleksandr Fomin, a Soviet diplomat, had told him that Khrushchev wanted a way out of the crisis. If the United States pledged never to invade Cuba, the Russians would dismantle their missiles and return them to the Soviet Union. A similar message had been communicated to veteran diplomat Averell Harriman who'd sensed the same willingness, but added that Khrushchev was under tremendous pressure from the right wing in his country to "teach the Americans a lesson."[3]

The following day, an American U-2 plane was shot down over Cuba, killing the pilot, Major Rudolf Anderson.

"This means war!" were the first words out of McNamara's mouth. Then, ExCom received a second message, supposedly from Khrushchev, stating that in order for the missiles to be dismantled, the U.S. would not only have to pledge not to invade Cuba, but also remove its missiles from Turkey. What did it mean?

This is when Robert Kennedy spoke out. If Harriman was right and Khrushchev was looking for a mouse hole to escape this situation, why not respond to Scali's personal proposal and just pretend the second was never received?

That's exactly what ExCom decided to do, and on the morning of Sunday, October 28, the White House learned that Khrushchev agreed to dismantle and withdraw the Cuban missiles. The crisis was over.

"In recent books and movies such as *Thirteen Days*, the 2001 thriller starring Kevin Costner," Gallagher speculates today, "the theory that a secret deal was cut between the Kennedys and Khrushchev to remove our Jupiter missiles from Turkey, which happened quietly six months later, has been given much credence, a theory that is eminently possible. And why not? Those missiles were obsolete and while they may have provided a psychological edge, their military importance was negligible, so that if you weighed one against the other—the Cuban missiles for those in Turkey—the U.S. came out the winner, both from a military and world opinion perspective."

To Gallagher, this was the most dangerous moment in the history of the world. The wrong decision from an insecure man could have destroyed most of the planet with hundreds of millions of casualties, mostly American, Soviet and European. Kennedy's managing of this crisis, Gallagher believes, was his finest moment.

THE PRIVACY WAR

# XIII
# The Death OF Civil Liberties

**"This all ended in the early afternoon of November 23, 1963."**

Gallagher's fourth year in Congress, 1962, came to a close with his star rising fast. Working with Kennedy's brother-in-law, Sergeant Shriver, he was one of the principal architects of the Peace Corps and the Arms Control and Disarmament Agency and had gained high visibility as floor manager, shepherding the passage of Kennedy's controversial $4.6 billion Foreign Aid Bill and $200 million United Nations bond issue. Aside from leading the Kennedy charge in the House, he had proven himself to be a worthy representative of United States in foreign affairs. Soon after, he was selected advisor to the Asian and Pacific Affairs Subcommittee and turned down the position of ambassador to Canada as well as a federal judgeship.

During that year, he and Rick were frequent guests at White House receptions marked by Jackie's penchant for superb French cuisine, stunning floral arrangements, sleek Casini evening gowns, bouffant hairdos and entertainment that heralded some of the world's premier artists including Carl Sandburg, Leonard Bernstein and Ella Fitzgerald. This was also the year that Rick gave birth to their fourth daughter, Bridget, and while one could say they were a glamorous couple and part of the

Kennedy in-crowd, Rick's German Lutheran upbringing and strong sense of fundamental values were the bedrock that kept it all in perspective.

In many ways, however, Gallagher stood out from the Washington crowd. He found himself constantly on the cutting edge, whether it was his beliefs over nuclear disarmament, standing up against the Russians or taking on bigotry and the government's abuse of power. He fought for individual rights and wanted a de-escalation of world tensions. He remained staunchly anti-Communist, but realized that in a nuclear age, the superpowers couldn't keep threatening all of the time, upping the ante, until war was the only way out. Without question, his stance on these issues earned him friends as well as enemies.

As the fall of 1963 approached, Bill Dawson, chairman of the Committee on Government Operations, finally took heed of Gallagher's pleas for formal inquiries into government intrusions into the private lives of American citizens and agreed to allow him to hold hearings. Almost immediately, newspapers from the *Washington Post* to the *Los Angeles Times* headlined him. As it turned out, formal hearings would not begin until one year later, but the pot was stirred.

As one of the chief proponents of civil rights since coming to Congress, Gallagher was delighted when African American activists from across the country held a testimonial dinner honoring him late that year. Attorney Ray Brown, who Gallagher had proposed to Kennedy when the new president wanted to nominate an African American lawyer to the federal bench in New Jersey, chaired the event. And in a letter about Gallagher's works with civil rights, Martin Luther King wrote, "Here is a perennial warrior of penetrating intensity . . . who does something about civil rights rather than merely talk about it."[1]

While the crowd of four hundred at the Hotel Plaza enjoyed speeches praising his stands on behalf of minorities by such individuals as Kennedy, Jesse Jackson and House Speaker McCormack, others were not so enthusiastic about his views on disarmament or the inquiries into governmental abuses. In October of that year, the Americans for Constitutional Action, a conservative group headquartered in Washington, D.C., rated him zero on a scale of one hundred, a distinction shared with just four other legislators in Congress.[2]

In June 1963, Gallagher attended a discussion between the president, Bobby Kennedy and Kenny O'Donnell about lining up support in the House for passage of the proposed Civil Rights Act. Later in their meeting, Gallagher found the president waving him over. Kennedy lit a cigar and they walked into the Rose Garden because, Gallagher knew, Kennedy was certain the Oval Office was bugged.

"You know," the president began. "Hoover has been tapping phones all over God's creation and tells me that two of Martin Luther King's aides are Communists. I don't know if it's true or not, neither does Bobby, but it complicates things. You want to support King and what he's trying to do, but he's a stubborn bastard. Even though we've warned him about them, he won't get rid of them. He says he trusts them, but he's not too sure about Hoover. Unfortunately, he's right."

"I wondered how that situation was going," said Gallagher. "I was talking to John Rooney the other day and he said, 'You and Chuck Joelson are pretty friendly, right?' So, I said 'yes' and he proceeded to tell me how Chuck, a member of Rooney's three-man subcommittee, dared to ask Hoover a question during his one yearly appearance before a congressional hearing. Directly afterward, Hoover collared Rooney and said, 'You tell that bastard to wise up or he'll have more trouble than he knows what to do with.' Since that day, Joelson can't go anywhere without two FBI agents following him. Can you imagine? All this because he had the audacity to ask one question."

Kennedy shook his head. "Tell me why that doesn't surprise me? But that's Hoover, a tough son of a bitch with a lot of information on everyone…even me."

Only later would Gallagher learn that Hoover's files on Kennedy included information ranging from tapes of a World War II romance between he and suspected East German spy Inga Arvad to photographic evidence of his affairs to confirmation gained from FBI wiretaps of his and Bobby's relationships with Marilyn Monroe.[3]

Of greater concern was an incident that surfaced two months later concerning a sexual encounter between Kennedy and Ellen Rometsch, an East German refugee who'd once been a member of the Communist Youth Organization. At the time, after FBI agents questioned her about relationships she had with high-level Washington politicians, with the cooperation of German authorities and an undisclosed amount of money given to her by Bobby Kennedy, she was quietly returned to Europe.

Unfortunately it didn't end there for the president. When the Senate Rules Committee learned of the Rometsch-Kennedy affair, Kennedy was forced to bare his soul to Hoover, asking him to use his leverage to stop her extradition. The director complied, saving Kennedy's good name and, in the short run, his presidency. But as with all deals with Hoover, there was a heavy price tag. Hoover would use the leverage to gain the authority to wiretap the phone and bug the residences of Martin Luther King regarding his suspicions about King's aides.[4]

It was a Faustian contract that some months later would ensnare both Bobby Kennedy and Gallagher. How could the attorney general, a vocal proponent of civil rights, hope to control Hoover once he'd agreed to spy on King? More to the point, how could John Kennedy hope to survive now that the director saw the chief executive of the United States as susceptible to blackmail by Mafia figures and a target for Soviet espionage after his affair?

In his final days, there was a profound change in the president, Gallagher noticed. In early August 1963, Jackie underwent emergency caesarian surgery and gave birth to Patrick Bouvier Kennedy, five-and-a-half weeks premature, only to die two days later. Perhaps, it was Kennedy's latest trip to the brink of mortality during the Cuban Missile Crisis or a coming to grips with his own moral lapses, but his self-absorption and detachment, which left one with the impression of a "history professor lecturing the class, but thinking all the while of his next book,"[5] evaporated with Patrick's death. This left him more human, and certainly more vulnerable. When the baby died, Jack wept bitterly. "An agonizing moment," it was according to Cardinal Cushing, "for a man never known to have had an emotional outburst."[6]

Beyond this personal evolution, Kennedy had hit his stride in terms of what he felt was important, not just for the United States, but for the world. He was an idealist and no longer feared the political swipes of the right wing who had taunted him through both the Cuban Missile Crisis and Bay of Pigs as a Cold War crusader and a politician who lived in a world of TV images. He battled valiantly on behalf of civil rights for African Americans in the South with specific actions such as his federalizing of the National Guard in Alabama in September while putting forward to Congress the broader, more sweeping Civil Rights Act of 1963. Clearly, a substantive change had occurred regarding his views on the Soviet Union, declaring in a June 28, 1963 speech before a joint session of Irish Parliament "there are no permanent enemies."[7]

He followed that bold proclamation with the opening of nuclear test-ban talks in Moscow and the signing of a test-ban pact just twenty days later. In fact, during the last six months of his presidency no fewer than one-half of his speeches involved either support for civil rights or the quest for world peace, eventually bringing on a thirty-minute address to the UN General Assembly calling for a joint U.S.-Soviet expedition to the moon. But this all ended in the early afternoon of November 23, 1963.

Minority Leader Bob Michael ran into Gallagher's office. "Jesus, Jack's been shot! I just heard it on the radio."

"What? Where did it happen?" Gallagher asked.

"Dallas. He was there campaigning with Connally."

"Well, I guess that will guarantee his reelection," he quipped, soon realizing that this was no joke. Though the initial report mentioned just one shot, it dawned on him that even serious wounds would be minimized in the interest of national security. "Where's the goddamned radio?"

Almost by the moment, reports on the president's condition became more grave, until Gallagher's secretary rushed in. "It's urgent," she said. "Speaker McCormack wants you in his office now."

When Gallagher arrived, a crowd of news people had already converged demanding a statement from McCormack who was number two in line behind Johnson for the presidency. Gallagher pushed his way into the office surprised to find only House Majority Leader Carl Albert; Carl Vincent, Chairman of the Armed Services Committee; and a growing tide of Secret Service agents gathered around his large mahogany desk.

"I just received a call from Parkland Memorial in Dallas," said McCormack. "Nobody expects the president to live."

The news struck Gallagher like a lightning bolt. "We need to issue some kind of statement to the press."

"No," McCormack said, staring at the silent black phone. "You write something for me and deliver it. I'm going to stay right here until we get some final news on Jack and Lyndon."

Gallagher and John Monahan, McCormack's secretary, composed a short statement regarding the president's condition, but by the time it was written, final word had come. John F. Kennedy was pronounced dead at 1:00 P.M.

Afterward, McCormack asked Gallagher to drive out to Andrews Air Force Base with him to meet the plane carrying the president's body. It was McCormack, Speaker Carl Albert, Carl Vincent and Gallagher. They took the speaker's car. It was getting dark, with thousands of mourners walking along the road. Since their car was an official one, they could weave through the traffic with police cars leading the way. The scene was tragic. Cars were abandoned and people walked dazed in the direction of Andrews.

When they arrived, they were asked to wait while microphones were set up near the tarmac. Gallagher then noticed an oil tanker off thirty or forty feet from where they were standing. He then saw a man pacing beside the tanker. It was Bobby. Gallagher walked over and put his arm around him as the two men paced together. Bobby was crying. Gallagher said nothing.

Once *Air Force One* landed, Bobby joined Jackie, who'd deplaned, followed by Lyndon Johnson, now in tears. He spoke with McCormack before finally walking to the microphones where he made a short statement to the press, later inviting McCormack and others to join him at the White House. The new president turned and walked toward the waiting helicopter.

"Say," Gallagher called out to a short, black-haired man about to leave with Johnson and McCormack. He turned. It was Jack Valenti, Johnson's aide. "Maybe the president should invite McCormack to fly back with him. I'm sure they've got a lot to discuss."

Valenti agreed, but when invited, the House Speaker, who had a fear of helicopters, declined. So McCormack, Carl Albert and Gallagher headed back to the White House by car.

Who or what could possibly be behind the assassination, they wondered. Was it the Russians? Castro? A right-wing zealot? Was the government's leadership under attack? The answer would follow mere hours later when at 7:10 P.M., a small group of them watched Walter Cronkite report that Lee Harvey Oswald had been formally charged with the assassination.

The preliminary theory was compelling. Oswald, a self-proclaimed Marxist, had spent time in the Soviet Union and had campaigned on street corners on behalf of Castro. He had been photographed holding the assassination weapon weeks before, which had been traced to him through a Chicago mail-order house after fleeing the scene of a second murder, which had left a Dallas police officer mortally wounded.

"Well, I guess they've got him," Valenti commented. "Tragic to think that a person of Jack's stature could be cut down in his prime by someone like that. But I suppose it's better than World War III."

"Absolutely," agreed Johnson, only now beginning to feel the weight of his new role. "The trick is to get the investigation behind us. I spoke with Hoover and we concur. Study it. Draw up the papers, then close the son of a bitch down. The sooner, the better, if only to keep the country from dwelling on this horrible tragedy."

Gallagher didn't sleep that night. It seemed incomprehensible that the president of the greatest country on Earth could be snuffed out, that security wouldn't have been better. But he would soon see the world that existed behind the curtain. And if he had any doubts that the truth about Jack's assassination resided far deeper than the Lee Harvey Oswald lone assassin theory, they would not be allayed. In the months to come, Oswald, Martin Luther King, Robert Kennedy and Hale Boggs would all be murdered or would die under circumstances similarly suspicious to Gallagher. It was these suspicions that would later place him head-to-head with Hoover in a battle that would, in many ways, help shape the framework of American society as we know it today.

# THE PRIVACY WAR

# XIV
# The Televised Assassination

**"It was Hoover's people that put Ruby there."**

Twenty-four million people watched Jack Ruby shoot and kill Lee Harvey Oswald on national television. Within seven days, President Lyndon Johnson created the Warren Commission to assess the possibility of a conspiracy.

While Johnson's motives seemed pragmatic, the same cannot necessarily be said for Hoover. In a telephone conversation with White House aide Walter Jenkins, the director confided, "The thing I am most concerned about…is having something issued so we can convince the public that Oswald is the real assassin."[1]

On November 24, only hours before Ruby shot Oswald, Attorney General Nicholas Katzenbach echoed those same sentiments in a memo sent to Johnson's press secretary Bill Moyer.

"The public must be satisfied that Oswald was the lone assassin, that he did not have confederates who are still at large and that the evidence was such that he would have been convicted at trial. Speculations about Oswald's motivation must be cut off."[2]

That same day, Alan Belmont, who headed the FBI's Kennedy assassination investigation, wrote to Clyde Tolson. He was sending two headquarter supervisors to Dallas to "review the investigative findings of our agents on the Oswald matter, so that we can prepare a memorandum to the attorney general setting out the evidence showing that Oswald is responsible for the shooting that killed the president."³

Why this obsession with speed, Gallagher wondered. Why this need to conclude and effectively terminate the investigation of the killing of the President of the United States before it had even begun? Why was Hoover in such a hurry to see Oswald proclaimed the "lone assassin," and why, too, was he so relieved at the brevity of his national exposé?

The answers to some of Gallagher's questions became apparent one afternoon in late December 1963 when he ran into Hale Boggs in the Members' Dining Room in the Capitol. A member of the Warren Commission, Boggs asked to meet with him privately. An hour later, the two stood in a deserted corner of the House lobby comparing notes on the progress of the investigation. He'd never seen anything like what had been going on in the Warren Commission.

"Do you know that every afternoon after our hearings," Boggs said, "Hoover is strong-arming members into briefing him on secret testimony and questions the commission will be asking the FBI in advance? He tried to do the same to me, but I told him I wanted no part of it."

"Those are closed sessions," Gallagher remarked.

"You bet they are, but this thing has been wired. The report the FBI provided us leaves a million questions. There's not a piece of information in it that hasn't already appeared in the press and one hell of a lot that's been left out. Soon I'm going public with everything that's gone on with Hoover and the FBI. There's evidence, discarded now, brought up that Oswald was a paid informant of the FBI."

Boggs went on to explain that, being personal friends with

Jim Garrison from his college days at Louisiana State University, he learned that Oswald met with crime figures and two CIA operatives months before the assassination to discuss killing John Kennedy, but the commission had no interest in meeting with him.

"I intend to stand up to them." Boggs vowed. "You can't have a government run by the FBI and CIA. That's not what democracies are about and, mark my words, soon you and your Privacy Subcommittee are going to come to the same conclusion, whether you want to or not."

When confronted with the allegations, Hoover flatly stated that neither Oswald nor Ruby had ever been FBI informants, though it was subsequently learned that Oswald's address book had contained the name of one FBI agent, that a note from Oswald to him had been destroyed and that the FBI had no fewer than nine contacts with Jack Ruby.[4]

Of all the appointments involved with the inquiry, it was Allen Dulles who was the most suspicious to Gallagher. Why would an ex-CIA director, who was fired by Kennedy and was his archenemy, be appointed to investigate his death and the possible involvement of the agency he had run unless people high up in the government wanted to preclude the possibility of a conspiracy finding? Though this all seemed very strange to Gallagher, it wasn't until years later that he came upon the most stunning piece of evidence of all.

Gallagher stopped to talk to one reporter who was at the scene of Oswald's shooting. "What a stroke of good fortune," Gallagher mentioned to him. "There couldn't have been too many reporters that even knew about the route Oswald was taking, so how were you so lucky to be there at exactly the right place and time to cover the story?"

"Well, Jack Ruby was there, too, right?" he asked. "So, how

did a guy like that get in?"

He paused for effect.

"I'm going to tell you something that I wouldn't dare to write. It was Hoover's people that got Ruby those credentials. It was Hoover's people that put Ruby there."

The conclusion Gallagher drew at the time was incontrovertible. Directly or indirectly, Gallagher believes, it was the FBI that arranged the shooting that would forever prevent Lee Harvey Oswald from telling the truth about his involvement in the assassination of John F. Kennedy.

# XV
# The Polygraph Hearings

**"We have not only invaded the walls of a man's castle with surreptitious surveillance, bugs and eavesdropping paraphernalia, but now are invading his mind."**

Without question, these were convoluted times, even by cold war standards. The volatile issues of the signing of the Gulf of Tonkin Resolution escalating the war in Vietnam and detonation of Communist China's first nuclear device roiled beneath the surface. But nowhere was the juxtaposition of what America wanted to be versus what it was more evident than in the cinema. Moviegoers admired Audrey Hepburn in *My Fair Lady* and delighted at Julie Andrews in *Mary Poppins*. In the theater next door, others gnawed nails with Henry Fonda in *Fail Safe* while laughing, albeit skittishly, at Peter Sellers' antics in Stanley Kubrick's dark comedy *Dr. Strangelove or: How I Learned To Stop Worrying and Love the Bomb*.

So it was during this time of ambiguity that Gallagher's privacy war grew more and more popular with the issue of polygraph testing from a government operations inquiry into a full-blown national debate and subcommittee hearing. Well known as a close friend of the slain President and champion of Kennedy causes, it was not uncommon for he and Rick to be written up in

Washington gossip columns. They played tennis at Hickory Hill, Bobby Kennedy's Virginia estate, and attended cocktail parties with RFK's favorite reporter Sandy Vanocour, Sergeant and Eunice Kennedy Shriver, singer Andy Williams and his wife, actress Claudine Longet.

Given some modest talent and the pro-RFK sentiments that rang through the country at the time, it surprised no one when newspapers outside of the New Jersey and New York area began touting Gallagher as a vice presidential prospect. Even more telling was the national uproar unleashed by his "Use of Polygraphs by the Federal Government" hearings on Capitol Hill. Begun with articles in local New Jersey papers and fueled by accounts of abuse of the device, a firestorm of outrage spread through the media. When the hearings mentioned the episode of Theresa Miller, it sent a shockwave through the country.

The use of a lie detector as a condition of employment was growing in the federal government. Some job applicants, including some workers, had been subjected to tests without their knowledge, not only by the Pentagon but by many federal agencies. Regardless of this blatant violation of the Fourth Amendment, the methodology of lie-detecting had been found to be inaccurate. Gallagher advocated legislation to set up minimum standards for polygraph operators because they, he claimed, were the real lie detectors.

Soon after, *Business Week* ran a multi-page pictorial previewing the latest in clandestine surveillance equipment with the story. The article cited examples of multimillion-dollar technology-information thefts perpetrated through the use of wiretapping, bugs and two-way mirror surveillance. Following was a steady stream of public protests against mail stops, or the temporary confiscation and illegal monitoring of the mail of private U.S. citizens. Also protested were illegal wiretaps, "black bag" break-ins, or covert break-ins and burglaries into private residences, and witness tampering by the Department of Justice against Jimmy Hoffa.

Since privacy was becoming such a major issue, Congress was ready to do something about it. It was in this post-assassination, post-Warren Commission, who-is-spying-on-whom environment that Gallagher opened the much-anticipated April 7-9 1964 House Information Subcommittee Hearing with a scathing rebuke of the Civil Service Commission's handling of the now-famous Theresa Miller affair.

"I am demanding to be allowed to personally cross-examine Director John W. Macy about the Theresa Miller incident and dozens of other abuses that have since been brought to my attention," Gallagher said. "Further, I intend to require of Mr. Macy a full account of how lie-detection devices are used, why they are used and where the results of that testing ultimately reside."

The Committee Chairman was stunned and, though he could have granted Gallagher's request, staunchly refused to call Macy as a witness.

"If that's your decision, Mr. Chairman," Gallagher said, "if you will not allow duly authorized investigators the latitude to investigate these government abuses, I charge this committee with perpetrating a whitewash. The fact is, lie detection devices are routinely being used to screen government applicants, test the loyalty of government workers in non-sensitive positions and help determine motive, as was the case with every free Cuban American who enlisted in the army this year."

Meeting with reporters before television cameras hastily set up in the Hearing Room corridor afterward, Gallagher was more explicit.

"These hearings are a sham. The $5 million per year polygraph industry is growing at alarming rates not only in the federal government, but in private industry where there are now 500 firms, employing 1,500 polygraph examiners, screening applicants and current employees 80 percent of the time just to see if they are honest. In the United States today we have progressed so far scientifically that we have not only invaded the walls of a man's castle with surreptitious surveillance, bugs and eavesdropping paraphernalia, but now are invading his mind. Ultimately, there must be a Supreme Court decision to clear the air in this undefined legal area. Meanwhile, we need some legislation."

Afterward, with the larger issue of individual rights brought to the fore, Gallagher's next move was to put forward a series of sensible legislative solutions. Existing laws governing the use of wire taps and other listening devices were made uniform. New regulations governing the use of hidden cameras and establishing minimum training standards for polygraph operators were written into law. And a review of regulations that permitted law enforcement's use of mail stops was undertaken.

Within three months, Gallagher's efforts yielded hard results. Spurred by the committee's release of a previously top-secret State Department study calling into question the efficacy of polygraphs, the use of lie-detection devices was stopped by all government agencies with exception of the CIA, Department of Defense and State Department. Reacting to the public furor over the privacy issue, Gallagher was named chairman of a special three-man House subcommittee established "to learn whether any government agencies were invading the privacy of Americans in possible violation of their constitutional rights."[1]

# XVI
# The CIA and Personality Manipulation

## "This was the method to select a perfect killing machine."

In truth, Gallagher didn't know what he'd stumbled onto. His agenda was filled with the struggle for meaningful civil rights legislation, taking care of his constituency in New Jersey and his true love, foreign affairs, not the illegal tapping of phones and domestic spying. He was, at that time, already a member of the Foreign Affairs and Government Operations Committees, chairman of the International Organizations and Movements Subcommittee, and a member of the Asian and Pacific Affairs Subcommittee, working closely with the president during the height of the Vietnam War.

In retrospect, Gallagher wonders what would have happened if he'd only gone home early the evening that Theresa Miller and her mother stepped into the Old Congressional Building. No one can know, but one thing is certain. What happened to Theresa Miller with polygraphs and to Mary Gunder-Mullenhof with personality testing set off a firestorm among the population, not only with politicians or the media, but with people like those who Gallagher represented in Jersey City and Bayonne and in cities and towns across the nation.

Certainly, few, if any, knew about the twenty-five years the

CIA had secretly devoted to behavioral-control programs using combinations of chemical and electrical stimulation to the brain in search of a programmed assassin to be used for executive-action-type operations. Having gained access to CIA Office of Research and Development files, Gallagher learned that programs were underway on "behavioral research including operational activities related to bio-electrics, radio stimulation of the brain, electronic destruction of memory, stereotaxic surgery, hypnotism, microwaves and ultrasonic."[1] The result involved paradigm-shattering breakthroughs in Radio-Hypnotic Intra Cerebral Control and Electronic Dissolution of Memory.

"We looked at the manipulation of genes and even gene splintering," claims one technical services staff researcher. "The rest of the world didn't ask until 1986 the type of questions we were facing in 1963. Everybody was looking to build a super-soldier who would take orders without questioning, like the kamikaze pilot. Creating a subservient society was not out of sight."[2]

While an ex-CIA psychologist saw personality testing as a method of assessing human inadequacies and strengths to be used in tailor-made harassment, others saw it as a method to select a person who could dissociate personality from the main body of consciousness. In other words, this was the method to select a perfect killing machine.[3]

The early experiments, Gallagher learned, many of them permanently mind-altering, were carried out on prisoners who were usually rewarded with heroin or other drugs at the California Medical Facility at Vacaville, the Addiction Research Center in Lexington, Kentucky, and even well-established hospitals like Georgetown University Hospital in Washington.

Gallagher also learned that powerful drugs were tested on terminal cancer patients and mentally ill patients as part of the

CIA's MKSEARCH initiative, successor to the MKULTRA mind-control initiative. At the Allan Memorial Hospital Institute in Montreal, an anonymously named patient named Mary C. was left in a sensory deprivation box for thirty-five days straight as part of a CIA experiment to depattern the brain. In other experiments in their unremitting attempt to create a state of artificially induced amnesia, subjects were lobotomized and then placed in the box for protracted periods in order to study the effects of sensory deprivation on lobotomized individuals.

As early as the late 1950s, Gallagher discovered, experiments were conducted in hypnosis to create a programmed assassin. One person tested was a secretary who was put into a deep trance and told to keep sleeping until ordered otherwise. Then a second secretary was hypnotized and told that if she could not wake up her friend, she would be so full of rage that she would not hesitate to kill. A pistol was left nearby, which the secretary had no way of knowing was left unloaded. Even though she had earlier expressed a fear of firearms, she picked up the pistol and pulled the trigger on her sleeping friend. After Allen brought her out of her trance, she denied that the event occurred and claimed that she would never shoot anyone.[4]

Just as mind-boggling to Gallagher, given the motives behind personality testing, were the personality profiles of both Oswald and Ruby and their reactions after committing their murders. Both were misfits, detached, eerily disconnected from their victims and from the violent acts they perpetrated. Oswald, the navy man, Soviet defector, and self-styled revolutionary, called himself a patsy from the moment he was captured, and even Hoover in his discussion with Johnson on the subject seemed frustrated at the fact that interrogation had yielded little. "This man Oswald has still denied everything. He doesn't know anything about anything."[5] Odd,

Gallagher believed, for a man trying to find his way into the history books. If that's what he was after, why deny it?

Ruby, on the other hand, was a police groupie, a sometime FBI informant and small-time Mafia operative whose motive for killing Oswald was his proclaimed love for the president and his grief over Jackie Kennedy's suffering. Was this really a motive, Gallagher wonders.

Dr. Roy Schafer, clinical professor of Psychiatry at Yale University, noted in court testimony that something had "affected Ruby's ability to control his own actions. He appears to feel not altogether in control of his body actions as if they occurred independently of his conscious will at times."[6]

Exactly whose doors was Gallagher knocking on by the end of 1964? Having won re-election by more than 63,000 votes, with an ever-escalating war blazing in Southeast Asia, racial rioting all around the nation and the Peoples Republic of China now armed with nuclear weapons, to him there appeared yet another front to fight, another enemy to conquer. Only this time, it wasn't Hitler, Ho Chi Minh, Brezhnev or Mao, but the man Gallagher believes was behind all this: J. Edgar Hoover.

# XVII
## Operation Phoenix and COINTELPRO

**"...atrocities in Vietnam, perpetrated, not by the Viet Cong, but by CIA agents."**

As 1964 ended, Gallagher aggressively promoted the three cornerstones of Lyndon Johnson's presidency: the great society, civil rights and a strong stand against Communism in Vietnam. Having just come off a landslide election which saw him capture 61.1 percent of the popular vote, Johnson's view of himself as the heir to Kennedy's legacy persisted. It was he who'd been elected this time, on his own, and he was hell bent now to turn into reality the vision of America he wanted to create. It was an America based largely on the humanitarian outlook of his idol FDR and molded during his childhood and adolescence where he, like those he envisioned helping, grew up a boy of modest means in rural Texas.

Working closely with the president on Medicare, the Voting Rights Act of 1965 and Southeast Asian policy, Gallagher had genuine insight not only into Johnson's actions, but the incidents that made him the president he became, the most compassionate president in his view, perhaps since Lincoln. He fought the hardest of any man he knew, including JFK, to protect civil liberties and was obsessed with helping the average American and in particular, the poor.

Poverty was in his background. His father, Sam Johnson, was a six-term member of the state legislature and used to take Lyndon along with him as a boy to campaign. Back then, legislators weren't full time. They'd earn a couple of dollars a day when in session, but it was a token, and the family's real income was generated from the cotton his dad grew on the farm that he owned and worked.

This was a man who, for his time, was extremely progressive. Sam Johnson took a bold stand against the Ku Klux Klan and personally lent money to families where the husband had lost his job or were in danger of losing their home to the banks.

"Did you ever see a person who was embarrassed?" Gallagher asks today. "Not about something they had done, but by how they looked, or about the neighborhood they lived in, or what their father did for a living? That's how Lyndon was. Here was a fifty-eight-year-old man still deeply troubled by the fact that cotton prices dropped and his father went bankrupt. It bothered him to that day and, I think, fueled the almost manic energy he showed in passing legislation."

Gallagher shared this quality with Johnson. He believed that the credibility of the United States was at risk not only with its allies, but also with the Soviets and especially China. Kennedy's stand against the USSR during the Cuban Missile Crisis demonstrated the U.S. resolve to face even nuclear war in order to halt Communist aggression. This was the lesson that Khrushchev learned and passed along to his successors.

But in the case of China, no such catharsis had happened, so Mao, in Gallagher's view, appraising the outcome of the Korean War and construing it as victory, saw the United States as a lazy, uncommitted nation. This view of Gallagher's was reinforced when the United States abandoned strategically important military bases in Laos two years earlier so that Mao, who was dying, and his Gang of Four, who were hardcore militarists, believed they could strong arm and eventually defeat the United States in battle. To Gallagher, at that moment, it was essential that the United States show resolve in an indirect conventional confrontation over Vietnam, much as it had done in Cuba, or risk a direct and potentially catastrophic nuclear showdown later, on their terms.

Despite his backing of LBJ's Vietnam policy intellectually, there was an ugliness erupting. By mid-1965, photos of college-age protesters being led away in handcuffs painted the front pages of nearly every newspaper in the country. Even more perplexing, during visits to camps outside Saigon, as chairman of Asian Affairs, Gallagher had begun hearing rumors, disturbing and lurid, about atrocities in Vietnam, perpetrated, not by the Viet Cong, but by CIA agents. Disguising themselves as the enemy, Gallagher learned, they would rampage through peasant villages at night, raping women and executing their husbands, allegedly as a matter of policy.

Then there was the matter of telephone harassments of the families of soldiers fighting in Vietnam. One such incident involved Captain James D. Strachen. Strachen's mother received a call from a woman who refused to give her name. She asked Mrs. Strachen to join a group with the intent of getting the soldiers out of Vietnam. Mrs. Strachen kindly declined and explained that though she wanted her son home, she wanted him to stay until the job was finished. The caller then said that if that was the way she felt, she looked forward to her son being killed in combat.[1]

Another incident involved Marine Lance Corporal Paul A. Devers of Jackson Heights, N.Y. He was killed in the war and his body was flown home for burial. Devers' brother, Peter, recalled that on the morning of the funeral at roughly 9 o'clock, the telephone rang. The man on the other end asked to speak to Josephine, his mother. He said he was a personal friend, but refused to give his name. He said that he wanted to tell her how very happy he was to hear that her son was killed. When Devers asked why, the man said it was because he was a card-carrying member of the Communist Party and that the soldiers were suppressing freedom in Vietnam. The man then threatened to kill her.[2]

The calls came frequently until the Devers family was finally forced to change its phone to an unlisted number. The families of other servicemen stationed in South Vietnam had been forced to do the same as a result of similar hostile phone calls.[3] Gallagher later discovered that the callers had been government agents and that he had had his first encounter with two of the CIA/FBI's darkest, most clandestine initiatives: Operation Phoenix and COINTELPRO.

Gallagher first learned about Phoenix in mid-1965 while on a tour of camps outside Vietnamese cities such as Hue where, firsthand, he would try to find out how the war was progressing and report back to Rusk and Johnson.

During the course of conversations with several young officers, one of them wondered aloud if some of the things the U.S. was doing to win the conflict were right or effective. He mentioned that people, soldiers like himself believed to be loyal in the villages and who they counted on in the day, often didn't make it through the night. The next morning when they went back to those villages, their friends would be murdered, often in the most horrible ways.

"Well, that ought to prove that the Viet Cong was pretty active," Gallagher said.

"No, you don't understand," the officer replied. "Not the Viet Cong. Us. The CIA. We're sending in assassination teams."

"What? Why would they be doing that?"

"Because someone had identified them as Cong operatives."

"Were they?"

"It's all really very confusing," the officer answered, looking down at his shoes.

It didn't take long to conclude that U.S. soldiers controlled certain villages by day. But by nightfall, these same people often turned into Viet Cong leaders.

The story stayed in Gallagher's mind and when he returned to Saigon that night and had a drink with some of the reporters at the Nationale Hotel, he first heard the name Operation Phoenix.

Gallagher immediately demanded a meeting with the station chief in Vietnam at the time. He told Gallagher that it was a program to kill the inhabitants of villages of untrustworthy Viet Cong leaders who claim to be friends.

"What if the reverse is true?" Gallagher asked. "What if the Viet Cong are fingering these guys who really are our allies and we're in there killing them? I mean, how much of this is going on?"

"Quite a bit," he said. "But we have to protect our people."

Gallagher was soon convinced that this was a massive campaign both in scope and brutality that was responsible by then for the murders of thousands of South Vietnamese citizens. Of course, he discussed the subject with Rusk and Johnson immediately upon his return to Washington. It was not until years later, however, while serving time in Schuylkill Prison, that Gallagher would come into possession of a document from a fellow inmate who was himself an assassin during the Phoenix program, which read:

> The Phoenix program is an essential element of Vietnam's
> defense against VCI subversion. While some unjustifiable abuses
> have occurred, as they have in many countries, the Vietnamese and

U.S. Governments are working to stop them, and to produce instead professional and intelligent operations which will meet the VCI attack with stern justice, with equal stress on both words. Considerable evidence has appeared from enemy documents that, despite some weaknesses, the program has reduced the power of the VCI and its prospects for conquest of the people of South Vietnam. Phung Hoang/Phoenix is as essential to the GVN's defense as the VCI is to the Communist attack. U.S. support is fully warranted.

As standard equipment most of us carried Hush Puppies, a Mark 22, Model 0, which used 9mm ammo and had a five-inch barrel equipped with silencer. This weapon, along with the fact that each of us could kill with our hands, had only one other thing in common—we were insane.

The most important element of the program, aside from the men, was the drugs supplied by the local Case Manager, that kept us awake for days at a time, erased the deeds committed from the mind and allowed peace to enter the soul, at least for a time. It was called the Green Hornet, a capsule containing a mixture of Benzedrine, an amphetamine which stimulated the central nervous system, Dexamil, a synthetic steroid with stimulated the adrenal gland, which made a man super-human, and Reserpine, commonly used to treat high blood pressure and mental patients.[4]

The Green Hornet that Jones described was a capsule that caused a man to act faster than normal. He could feel his heart speed up. The head would throb, and it felt as if the brain was actually growing. It gave the man his own personal radar, and his senses were fine-tuned to an extreme pitch. Every nerve ending was sensitive to sound, sight, and smell, and it seemed as if a receiver was in the brain. Put all this together, and a man could stay awake for days, fight, function, and not lose his mind.[5]

Lyndon Johnson and Gallagher debate Vietnam, the civil rights strategy and other matters in the Oval Office, 1965.

Kennedy, Gallagher, Johnson, after the Democratic National Convention, 1960

House Speaker McCormack with Gallagher and Wayne Hayes at the 1968
National Convention

The Jimmy Fair victory celebration, October, 14, 1962

Gallagher, in uniform, and John V. Kenney at an anti-Hague rally, Jersey City, 1951

Gallagher visits GIs as chairman of Asian affairs, Vietnam, 1968.

Gallagher, Frank Sinatra, Mayor Washington and Rep. Libonati (D-IL), Washington, D.C., 1968

Gallagher touring the village of Hue outside of Saigon

War correspondent Vince McMahan with Gallagher, Vietnam, 1967

Gallagher discusses Cuba with Secretary of State Herter, 1959

New Jersey delegation led by Gallagher, Democratic National Convention, Los Angeles, 1960

Gallagher with friend and mentor Mayor John V. Kenny, 1970

Gallagher speaking at the Capitol, 1965

Gallagher with President John F. Kennedy, April 1961

Gallagher, May, 1977

In 1965 the United States set a goal for the Phoenix Program to neutralize 20,000 agents during the year, and at the end of that year, 19,534 agents were reported neutralized. The figure was unsettling in that there had been no corresponding decline in American estimates of agents at large.[6]

Who, Gallagher then asked, were the 19,534 people, and what had become of them? As only 20 percent of those arrested were actually sentenced—and even then, only for a period of a few months—American officials concluded that a large percentage of the neutralized agents disappeared.[7]

Shortly after returning to Washington in mid-June 1965, Gallagher met with the president in his private office. Anxious to hear a firsthand report, Johnson seemed agitated as he loomed over his undersized desk contemplating a letter he'd recently received from Senate Majority Leader Mike Mansfield, an outspoken critic of the war.

Gallagher sat down knowing that what he had to tell the president was not such good news. The chair was small, and though he stood 6'1", sitting there made the already formidable president seem a lot larger.

"I've just been reading this note from Mansfield, which is interesting." The president began to read aloud. "'I do not conclude that our national interests are served by deep military involvement in Southeast Asia. If the decision must be for deeper involvement, I respectfully suggest that the basis for this be made much clearer and more persuasive to the people of this nation than has heretofore been the case.'" Johnson tossed the missive onto his desktop. "So what he's saying is get out, which we are not going to do." He sat back in his chair. "You ever milk a cow, Neil?"

"Can't say that I have, Mr. President."

"Well, let me tell you, Congressman, you take that bucket

and you put it under that cow, then, you work those teats careful and steady until that bucket is filled with the whitest, creamiest, best-looking milk you're ever going to find. Then, you look away, scratch your ass, or whatever and that cow's tail starts swinging, hits the mud and tosses a big piece of cow shit right on top of your creamy white milk. That's Mike Mansfield."

Gallagher laughed. "But I think he's got a point," he said. "If we're going to stay in this war, and if it's going to escalate, we're going to have to make people understand what's at stake. And frankly, Mr. President, from what I've seen it doesn't look good. The energy and persistence of the Viet Cong is astonishing. They can appear anywhere and at almost any time. They've accepted extraordinary losses and they come back for more."

"Yeah, but you have to wonder whether if you start some kind of education program in Laos and Cambodia and the rest now, if they're going to be hollering 'You're a warmonger!' And that's the horn the Republicans would like to get us on." The president shook his head. "If only we could do something in the way of social work, in the way of hospitals, in the way of our province program and remaking that area out there."

"That's one of the reasons I needed to see you, Mr. President. Do you know anything about the Phoenix operation going on out-side the camps, in the villages?"

"Phoenix?" The president thought for a moment. "Yeah, one of those CIA schemes, isn't it? Protect the loyal villagers from VC subversion or something like that. Why are you asking?"

Gallagher began to explain and the president sat back and lis-tened. "On the one hand, Mr. President, we talk about winning the minds and hearts of these people, and on the other, we're sending out teams of assassins to kill people we're not even sure are our enemy."

The president was furious. "You give them the go-ahead to

defend trustworthy villagers," he said, "and they take it as a free pass to run like a pack of wolves through the whole country. Here I am with Westmoreland wanting forty-four battalions of ground troops, McNamara wanting to bomb Vietnam's border with China and George Ball wanting to turn tail and run. The answer, I keep telling them, is not to start a nuclear war, or to run like cowards, but to keep a steady course. It's giving these people hope and something to fight for and putting some of our people into their units to do a better job fighting without material escalation for the next few months, that is what we need to do."

"That's right, but that's not what's happening and I'm afraid something serious could happen there and here in the U.S. if it ever got out."

"I agree. We can't have that going on and I'll see to it that those operations are stopped immediately."

Later that month, General Westmoreland did get his forty-four battalions of ground troops, bringing the total number up to 180,000. McNamara did get his saturation bombing, though Johnson would not allow it along the Chinese border. And the CIA, despite orders to the contrary, continued its efforts to purify South Vietnam of enemy agents, until 1972, arresting, torturing and killing more than 80,000 South Vietnamese citizens before the Phoenix operation was finally terminated.[8]

# THE PRIVACY WAR

# XVIII
# Joaquin Balaguer

**"This was the man to stabilize the government."**

One phone call that again led Gallagher dangerously close to the world of organized crime came from Joseph Zicarelli late in 1965, the effects of which would haunt him for the rest of his life. Still relatively new to the world of foreign affairs, he was focusing mainly on Berlin, Cuba and the Soviet Union, but in the end underlying even this conversation with Zicarelli was the issue of Communism, the Cold War and power. He remembers getting the call on the morning of September 5.

"I'd like to speak with you about something that might be of interest to the boys over at the State Department," Zicarelli said and went on to explain the situation of his friend, "a very prominent man in the Dominican Republic." The man was Joaquin Balaguer, the former interim president of the Dominican Republic, and he had received a pending order of deportation from the United States Department of Immigration. "He deserves help. He's a friend of the United States and I just want you to help keep this guy from getting deported."

Gallagher thought about it. Zicarelli apparently knew a lot of people, people who knew things that the Bissells and Rusks of the world simply couldn't. More compelling was that Zicarelli had been dead on target with his information about Soviet missiles in Cuba.

It was that conversation that first led the congressman to meet the diminutive, soft-spoken former Jesuit priest and his attorney. Impressed with Balaguer's intellect and sincerity, Gallagher later spoke on his behalf with the commissioner of immigration who had the order of deportation revoked on the condition that Balaguer not return to his native country. At that point, it was an all but forgotten issue. Leftist president Juan Bosch had been overthrown a year after his election and a junta was established.

Two years later, however, in 1965, when a group of liberal officers called Constitutionalists tried to oust the junta and restore Bosch, who was initially supported by the CIA, Lyndon Johnson ordered the 82nd Airborne to Santo Domingo to restore and supervise the election of a pro-democratic government. There seemed no one popular, or savvy, enough to quell the civil war, win the election and then rule with legitimate authority.

Then in March, 1966, with the Caribbean still reeling from Castro's takeover of Cuba and Communist rumblings throughout that area, Balaguer again contacted Gallagher, this time requesting that he be allowed to return to his native Dominican Republic. Since their first meeting, with the dispatch of American troops, Gallagher had familiarized himself with the situation and assessed the idea as viable. Balaguer was, by all accounts, an upstanding man, well-educated, with a loyal following and sincere desire to prevent bloodshed by stabilizing the government through democratically held elections. Wasn't this the kind of solution the State Department had been searching for?

Days later, Gallagher went to the White House to meet with President Johnson. Upon discussing the situation, the president called Rusk to arrange a meeting with Gallagher the next morning. At that time, Rusk asked Gallagher if it would be all right to place a State Department liaison officer with Balaguer to learn more about his intentions and ideas about the revolution. Gallagher later passed on word that Balaguer would have no objection. Shortly after, however, Balaguer again visited his office to say that the State Department liaison was ignoring his plight. Gallagher relayed the message and soon following, during a hearing before the Foreign Affairs Committee, the secretary sent a note asking that Gallagher meet with him privately at his car outside the building.

While sitting in his car, Rusk told Gallagher that, in his opinion, the State Department had "dropped the ball." He said that a survey had been done demonstrating that Balaguer was a powerful man in the Dominican Republic with a strong following. He asked Gallagher to speak to Balaguer and tell him that the United States would appoint a provisional president once the situation was stabilized, but it would not be him. However, if Balaguer and his constituency went along with the plan, open elections would be held in six to eight months and at that time he would be allowed to return to the Dominican Republic to run for president if he chose.

Later, in fall 1966, when free elections were announced, the provisional president, Cabral Reed, wanted to stay for the full term, and enormous pressure was put on the United States to keep Balaguer from returning to his native island. An intense debate took place within the administration as to what should happen in the Dominican Republic. At a meeting in the White House, Gallagher stressed that he had given Balaguer the president's word that if he did not make trouble for the provisional government he would be allowed to return.

The solution was found when Balaguer requested a temporary visit to return to the Dominican Republic to see his ailing mother. When Balaguer arrived at the Santo Domingo airport more than 50,000 cheering supporters were there to greet him and, later that year, in the second general election since the assassination of Rafael Trujillo, Balaguer was elected president.

Balaguer would be reelected four times more between 1978 and 1990. He was staunchly loyal to the United States government and to Gallagher for helping him return to his homeland until his death on July 14, 2002.

The turn of events leading to the election of Balaguer as president of the Dominican Republic would later be mentioned in a series articles published by *Life* magazine that linked Gallagher with the Mob, every charge of which has been proven untrue or without substantiation.

# XIX
# The Testing of Children

**"These tests are subject to distortion,
either purposefully or otherwise."**

Moving on with his commitment to the privacy war, Gallagher
learned that during the 1950s and 1960s, 500,000 children, grades
first, third, sixth, ninth and twelfth, were required to answer hundreds of questions about their personal lives as part of psychological
testing administered by the United States Department of Education.

> True or false:
>
> - My sex life is satisfactory.
>
> - There is something wrong with my sex organs.
>
> - Sexual things disgust me.
>
> - When a man is with a woman he is usually thinking about sex.
>
> - Evil spirits possess me at times.
>
> - I have never had black, tarry-looking bowel movements.
>
> - I am attracted to members of my own sex.
>
> - I read the Bible several times a week.
>
> - I deserve severe punishment for my sins.
>
> - Jesus Christ was savior of the world.[1]

Fill in the blank or answer the following:

- Who is now acting as your father?

- Where does the money come from that pays for your food, house and clothing?

- Think now about your parents' close friends. How many are white?

- About how often last year did your mother or father attend Parents' Association meetings like the PTA?

- My childhood was_____.

- My father_____me.

- God is _____.

- Men often _____women.

- Secretly I often dream of _____.

- My father's chief fault is _____.²


This information was required of schoolchildren, ages six through seventeen, throughout the United States. From then on, Gallagher learned, if an individual chose to work for the U.S. Government in a civil service position, tests far more searching were administered as a matter of course. Refusal meant no job.

At the time of Gallagher's Special Inquiry on the Invasion Of Privacy, the practice of using psychological testing increased 400 percent between 1964 and 1966 with no guidelines, restrictions or assurance of confidentiality.³

On June 3, 1966, following Gallagher's initial requests, John W. Macy was finally called before Reps. Benjamin Rosenthal, Frank Horton, and Henry Reuss and Gallagher to answer questions concerning the use of psychological testing by the Civil Service Commission. In a startling turn of events, once introduced, Macy read from a typewritten memorandum on the subject:

Personality tests of the type in question by the Committee fail to satisfy merit system precepts for Civil Service employment on a number of grounds: They were developed for clinical use and are not designed to measure the specific characteristics needed by persons working in particular occupations. These tests are subject to distortion, either purposefully or otherwise; therefore, the scores are undependable as a basis for employment decisions. The scores on such tests can easily be grossly misinterpreted and misapplied by persons who are not qualified psychiatrists or psychologists trained to interpret such test results.

In view of the character of the questions asked, if the results of personality tests are used for employment purposes, the individual's right to privacy is jeopardized.

For these reasons, Mr. Chairman, the Commission will no longer use or permit the use of personality tests in hiring civil service employees. I have issued a restatement of this policy to agencies to reaffirm and strengthen this position.[4]

Gallagher's subcommittee had won another rousing victory. With Macy's statement that morning the right to privacy for millions of civil service employees and job applicants was reclaimed. Soon enough, the State Department capitulated with dozens of other departments in a wave of bans on the practice.

Interestingly it was the Department of Education, among the most egregious in its use, that remained the most recalcitrant, saying on June 4, 1966, that "the safeguards against the abuse of questionnaires may be classified as 'professional,' 'institutional' and 'governmental.' In this connection, it deserves notice that the entire present governmental effort is coordinated by the Office of Statistical Standards, in the Bureau of the Budget. However, parental consent is another safeguard against the unjustifiable intrusion of privacy, and the Office of Education will also require this safeguard in all cases where it appears appropriate."[5]

In Gallagher's view, the Office of Education had no intention of stopping the testing or gaining parental consent for the use of the test. Second, it was the Office of Statistical Standards that would be collecting and maintaining the records for the millions of test results. It was clear to Gallagher that the Department of Education would be instrumental in supplying the results of psychological testing performed on students directly to the FBI and U.S. Army.

From a legislative standpoint, with regard to privacy, in 1966 Gallagher and his subcommittee were on a roll. In terms of polygraph testing, they'd won that battle with all but the Department of Defense, State Department and CIA. The same held true for psychological testing in the Civil Service Department, the largest in government. If the practice wasn't banned altogether, at least people understood that they couldn't be forced to take those tests, which had largely fallen into disrepute.

At that time, the Subcommittee on Privacy was also getting heavily involved in the investigation of IRS abuses and the plans for the National Data Bank Concept, a central database of information obtained from illegal wiretaps and other means from over twenty government agencies including the FBI and IRS, that abused the Forth Amendment right to freedom from unnecessary search and seizure. As a result of the privacy investigations two important acts were passed: the Freedom of Information Act and the Credit Reporting Act.

Gallagher expected opposition, but nothing could prepare him for what he found upon his return from a Florida vacation.

# XX
# Bugs

**"My phones are tapped, here in Washington**
**and at home in Louisiana."**

On March 23, 1966, at nine o'clock, the Gallagher family
arrived at their home. The lights were out and it was dark when
they entered. Gallagher unlocked the back door and Bridget and
Patti ran into the house. One by one, he flicked on the lights in
the kitchen and the foyer when suddenly Patti screamed. He and
Rick rushed to see what was wrong, their older daughters,
Diane and Chrissy, a half step behind. They stopped dead in their
tracks, seeing Patti and her younger sister frozen at the entrance
to the living room, which was ripped apart with the furniture
stripped and overturned, drawers torn from their sockets and
papers thrown everywhere.

Needless to say, Gallagher was alarmed, but knowing what
his work had led him to, he must have understood something of
what was going on. He ran immediately into the study where they
had a safe that contained financial records, birth certificates and
similar types of papers. Too stunned to follow, Rick walked around
the living room picking things up in a daze.

She muttered that they'd been robbed as the girls followed
her lead. Gallagher stormed back from the study.

"Don't touch anything until the police arrive," Gallagher said. "I want them to see that the safe was ripped open, but that nothing was taken."

When the police chief arrived with two Bayonne detectives, they examined the way the heavy gauge steel had been cut on the safe.

"We've seen this before, Congressman. This was no amateur. This type of cut requires a special tool only professionals would have access to."

The police called it a black bag operation. They said similar robberies were going on all over Hudson County at the time. The chief then told Gallagher something that shocked him. In his opinion, it wasn't thieves that had perpetrated this crime, but a government law enforcement agency, probably the FBI. This was when the depth of what he was taking on with his Committee's investigation into privacy really struck Gallagher.

"This is going to be like a war, isn't it?" Rick asked him later that night. "You're fighting the federal government, aren't you?"

"It never occurred to me that this could go so far."

Then in mid-September 1966, with a Senate committee also investigating privacy in full swing, Hale Boggs came by Gallagher's office for an impromptu meeting and told him that he had to talk about what was going on around Washington at the time.

Gallagher was sitting in his office going through some paperwork when Boggs walked in appearing very upset. "Neil, we need to talk about what's been going on around here lately." He sat down in one of the chairs in front of Gallagher's desk.

"I don't know what you're talking about, Hale."

"I'm talking about Hoover," Boggs said and leaned forward, his voice lowered. "I'm going to tell you something, Neil. I was on that Warren Commission and there's no way that Oswald killed

Jack by himself. No way. And I'm going to tell you something else. Hoover lied to the Commission about Oswald, Ruby, the bullets, the gun, you name it. It was a whitewash and I don't care who knows it. I want the investigation re-opened and Garrison has got the evidence to do it."

Gallagher then looked Boggs in the eye. "Hale, are you all right?"

"No," he answered. "Neil, I'm going to confide something to you that may make you think I'm crazy, but I know for a fact that my phones are tapped, here in Washington and at home in Louisiana. I also know that Hoover and the CIA have bugs planted in the House Caucus Rooms and most of our offices. A lot of us are being blackmailed, and I think it's high time we understood what we're up against."

Neither Boggs nor Gallagher could fully comprehend the extent of the surveillance practiced on thousands of unsuspecting American citizens by the FBI as part of their COINTELPRO initiative. At the time, having begun in the late 1950s, the FBI was actively involved in twelve separate counterintelligence programs according to Gallagher. Their tactics varied, but much like the CIA's "pick at the scabs" methodology, financial intimidation was a method of choice. During the known life of COINTELPRO, the IRS supplied the FBI with tax information on over a half million people and more than ten thousand organizations, many of which were targeted because of their political viewpoints or to settle personal vendettas.[1]

A chief source of investigative information that the FBI used was informers, very often troubled people, sexually or otherwise, whom agents would attempt to "turn" under threat of exposure or job dismissal. As one agent explained, "If we found out that so-and-so was one, and most of them were quite covert about their activities, that person would be 'doubled' and would become a listening post for the FBI. At the time, each agent had to have at least twenty-five informers reporting to him. An agent could also be awarded a money bonus if his informers' information became part of an indictment."[2]

Gallagher learned that other favored techniques used in COINTELPRO involved planting stories of crimes or serious accusations of fraud, drug use, criminal contacts, or embezzlement in newspapers, magazines and gossip columns. Sex usually played a role, and the FBI often, as with Martin Luther King, used tape recordings, anonymous letters or telephone calls to spread rumors about adultery, homosexuality or other sexual exploits. The informing of an employer, neighbors and friends that a target was a communist who was involved in terrorist activities or was a member of organized crime was one of the easiest and most widely used methods resulting in loss of employment, and/or emotional and financial destabilization, Gallagher claims. Planting evidence or removing it during black bag break-ins, requesting IRS audits and turning trusted friends into informers or "bait" in sting operations were all part of broad-based FBI initiatives that affected and often ruined thousands of unsuspecting American citizens during the years ranging from 1956 to 1971, the year COINTELPRO was officially terminated. Yet, though it was terminated officially, Gallagher attests that there is a great deal of evidence that suggests these practices continued in a variety of ways.

The next morning, Gallagher and Boggs met secretly with Speaker John McCormack and decided to have the corridors and offices of both houses of Congress swept for listening devices. To their chagrin a wiretap expert came back with a report that confirmed that a branch telephone line leading to cables in the White House, the Pentagon and congressional offices on Capitol Hill terminated at the Standard Oil Building at 26 Constitution Avenue where it was kept under lock and key. "One of the tenants of the top floor of this building," he later testified under oath, "is a Justice Department Agency.... The line lays open every congressman on Capitol Hill to the possibility of listening devices. Maybe it's the CIA, maybe it's the FBI, or some other organization listening in."

# THE PRIVACY WAR

# XXI
## Hoover's Enemies

**"Be on the lookout, Neil, because they're going to get you for this."**

By mid-1967, with anti-war demonstrations proliferating onto nearly every college campus and the nation's cities exploding, Lyndon Johnson was a man torn, haunted by John Kennedy's legacy and stalked by his living representative, Bobby, whose very name drove him to rage. Johnson wanted a nuclear non-proliferation treaty with the Soviets even then and later listed its signing on July 1, 1968, as among his most important accomplishments.

But Johnson's experience with World War II and the Cold War had taught him that aggression must be repulsed, so he believed defeat in Vietnam would unleash a Communist rampage across east Asia, even when CIA reports suggested otherwise. "I knew from the start," Johnson told Doris Kearns in 1970, "that I was bound to be crucified either way I moved. If I left the woman I really loved, the Great Society, in order to get involved with that bitch of a war on the other side of the world, then I would lose everything at home, all my programs. If I left that war and let the Communists take over South Vietnam, I would be seen as a coward and my nation would be seen as an appeaser and we would find it impossible to accomplish anything for anybody anywhere on the entire globe."[1]

It was in this environment, depressed and frustrated, with mass demonstrations taking place outside the White House that Gallagher met with Lyndon Johnson on the evening of March 17, 1967. Their conversation began on a personal note, but soon drifted toward the president's obsession: the Vietnam War.

"Neil, if you were in my chair, what would you do about this war that I'm not doing?" he asked. "I'm making these widows every day. I've got everybody screaming outside my door that I'm killing these kids and frankly, I don't know what else I can do to end this thing honorably."

"Well, let's say, you had a baseball team," Gallagher began. "You've got a beautiful stadium, the fans support you, but you can't win a game. Eventually, you start losing the fans' support even though you know you're going to win and you're on the right track. You need to do something to show that you understand their frustration and that you're doing something about it. You can't fire the team, but you can sure as hell change the manager."

"Neil, what are you talking about?"

"Our situation in Vietnam, Mr. President, is a little like that, don't you think? But now I'd like to talk about NATO in Brussels for a moment where they've got this huge Bentley. And that car, well, a man can walk straight into it without having to bend, without ever having to get dirty or wrinkle the crease on his trousers."

"Now, you've definitely lost me," said Johnson, who was having a little fun with the scenario.

"General Westmoreland is a man who would appreciate a Bentley, Mr. President. He's an excellent dresser, handsome in that uniform of his, all cleaned and pressed. Why don't you send him over to Brussels where he can walk into that Bentley without getting a wrinkle in his uniform and make him NATO commander?"

"Yeah, and who do I put in his place?"

"Mr. President, you've got one of the last of the great fighting generals of World War II, General Abrams, over there now as an observer. I believe he could do it."

"Is that so? And what makes you think he'd do any better?"

"Abrams is a straight shooter. He'd come back to you and say, 'Mr. President, this is what we have to do to win this war' or if we can't, he'd tell you how to get the hell out of there. It would be a new perspective instead of this rehashing of the same information you've been hearing over and over again. Abrams has the brains, the guts and the experience to call it for you."

The president sat back in his chair, digesting that for a moment, then egged him on. "What else?"

"Well, since we're on the subject, I don't think there's a better soldier anywhere than General Taylor. He was a fighting general who led the 101st, and I personally hold him in high regard. Still, he's been over there a long time and has become so involved that he may feel he needs to justify previous positions that he's advocated. Maybe it's time to have a new voice over there as ambassador, a realist who can take a hard look at what our choices really are."

"And I suppose you have a candidate in mind for that, too?"

"Ellsworth Bunker. He'll straighten out that problem in the Dominican Republic with the 82nd Airborne for you. He's old enough so he has no great political ambitions. If he was in Vietnam, he'd take a look and, like Abrams, give you a true assessment of what options there are, so you can make decisions with an objectivity that I don't believe you have right now."

"Neil, those are some damned good ideas and I thank you for them, but sometimes I really do wonder how all of this is going to end."

"It will end with history remembering you as the man who

held back Communism in Southeast Asia and prevented a nuclear war with China, Mr. President. Maybe not today, but that will be your legacy."

"You've heard what Bobby's been saying. For him to criticize the war now," Johnson fumed, shaking his head. "Well, I tell you if there had been no escalation, he would still be out there leading the fight against me, telling everyone that I'd betrayed John Kennedy's commitment to South Vietnam. He'd say I'd let a democracy fall into the hands of the Communists and that I was a coward. Oh, I can see that coming. You know, Neil, every night when I fall asleep, I see myself tied to the ground in the middle of a long, open space," he confided. "In the distance, I can hear the voices of people, thousands of them, shouting and running toward me: 'Coward! Traitor! Weakling!' It's either that, or this." He motioned outside the window toward the mob of demonstrators beyond the White House gates. "Not much of a choice, is it?"

Gallagher left Johnson that night with no commitment on any of his suggestions, though by mid-year the president had implemented them all. Then, as he was leaving, Gallagher remembers now, he couldn't help but glance back to see Johnson, still in his chair, pondering the war, the demonstrators and the ghost of John F. Kennedy. Of the three, the one he could never seem to reconcile was the betrayal he perceived in Bobby's split with him over a war that, ironically, he'd inherited from Jack Kennedy's best and brightest.

Tough times were not confined to Johnson's White House however. By 1967 the ever-escalating civil rights movement of 300,000 strong, led by Martin Luther King, began to fragment into less patient voices, condoning violence as a means to racial equality. Three years before when King won the Nobel Peace

Prize, J. Edgar Hoover mounted a full-scale campaign to neutralize the civil rights leader. The intensity of hatred he had for King was chilling. The only relationship that may have rivaled it was that between Hoover and Bobby Kennedy.

Badly shaken and horribly depressed after Jack's assassination, the attorney general was out in public for the first time visiting an orphanage where a Christmas party was being held. Assembled in the playroom of the orphanage, the children were playing until he entered and then, as they understood that this was the arrival of an important man, the children stopped playing. There wasn't a sound, and as Bobby observed them uncomfortably, surrounded by administrators, one boy, a six-year-old, ran up to him and cried out, "Your brother's dead! Your brother's dead!" Of course, everyone was stunned. The boy obviously meant no harm, but probably wanted simply to demonstrate to his teacher that he remembered a fact they'd all been taught. Nevertheless, the room was awash with disapproval and the boy, sensing this, began to cry. It was then that Bobby smiled gently, leaned down, gathered the boy up in his arms and hugged him as if he were his own. "It's all right," Bobby said. "I have another brother."[2]

This encounter had much to do with why Bobby became a man more feared after his brother's death, once he let his humanity show, than before when he was seen as his brother's keeper. Having received Last Rites from the Catholic Church on no fewer than five occasions, Jack Kennedy suffered with Addison's disease and immune system deficiencies for his entire life, so mortality and pain to him were constant companions.

After November 23, 1963, Bobby the absolutist, who knew everything, knew nothing. Without Jack his life must have seemed without meaning, his depth of loss insurmountable. He threw himself even more ferociously into the void, trying to fill it by becoming Jack. Helping to raise Carolyn and John Jr. as a surrogate father became an obsession to the point where his wife, Ethel, was forced to put her foot down. He wore his brother's clothing: a cashmere sweater, a tweed overcoat, a leather jacket from Jack's PT boat days.

It was no coincidence that Bobby's reading habits altered, too. The young firebrand transformed into a sensitive, thinking man preoccupied no longer with "get 'em" teams, but instead with the plays of Shakespeare, poems of Robert Lowell and essays of Ralph Waldo Emerson. Of particular interest was Edith Hamilton's The Greek Way and the works of existentialist philosophers like Sartre and Camus, his favorite quote coming from the dark, fatalism of the novel, The Plague. "Perhaps we cannot prevent this world from being a world in which children are tortured. But we can reduce the number of tortured children."[3]

As a New York senator, having broken ranks with Lyndon Johnson over the war, Bobby began to recognize that he had much to learn from the least fortunate of his fellow Americans and he seemed to grasp that his insulated Kennedy upbringing may have been too protective. "If I hadn't become a United States senator, I'd rather be working in Bedford-Stuyvesant than any place I know," he assured the audience in a meeting concerned with the disadvantaged Brooklyn neighborhood. "I wish I'd been an Indian," he told the Comanche wife of a Senate colleague. "If I hadn't been born rich, I'd probably be a revolutionary," he said to a reporter from Latin America. "I'm jealous of the fact that you grew up in a ghetto. I wish I'd had that experience,"[4] he informed journalist Jack Newfield, a native of Brooklyn. This was the Bobby Kennedy that was feared, not only by Johnson, but also by Hoover, both of whom saw in this newly evolved Kennedy a true political threat to the presidency of 1968.

Also, the bond between Hoover and Cohn, who had his own score to settle with Bobby, once again took hold. What would the world look like with Bobby as president? Hoover had an idea from when he was attorney general, some of the most miserable days of his life. Cohn had been feeling the sting of Kennedy's vengeance as the target of non-stop Department of Justice investigations during the previous several years. The very notion was intolerable, so the question became, How could they conspire to bring down one of the most popular figures of the time?

Gallagher remembers receiving a call from Cohn well in advance of Bobby's decision to run for president. Cohn told him it was important that he meet with a friend of his from the Teamsters who had substantive information regarding privacy abuses perpetrated by people at the highest levels of government, which could become the basis for an entire series of hearings. Gallagher, of course, agreed to the meeting.

Cohn's friend came into Gallagher's Washington office the following Tuesday. A good-looking, self-assured individual, he carried a suitcase filled with documents and said that Cohn explained to him that he was the man to come to about civil liberties issues. In his suitcase, he said Gallagher would find documents demonstrating abuse of power by the federal police against dozens of individuals, and that it was his for the taking to use as the basis of his subcommittee hearings.

He then left and Gallagher started sifting through the material. It was devastating: wiretapping, IRS coercion, witness tampering, all aimed at Bobby and the strike force concept during his tenure as attorney general. Noticeably absent, however, was any FBI involvement or references to the most obvious target: Jimmy Hoffa. In other words, whoever had put the documents together, Gallagher asserts, didn't want it discredited as an anti-Kennedy plot by the Teamsters.

"Man, this is dangerous stuff," he told the man the next day when he came by his office. "Where the hell did you get this?"

"You don't have to worry about that," he answered. "It's yours now and that's all that you need to know."

"But it is my concern. How do I know it's authentic? You can't think I'm going to take this without knowing who got it or how. In case you haven't figured it out, that's the basis of the privacy hearings."

"Well, I've been told that you'll accept it, no questions asked."

"Is that so? Told by whom?"

"Mr. Cohn."

Gallagher was infuriated. He handed the suitcase back to the man and demanded that he leave, saying that Cohn didn't run his office.

The man left and, of course, the next morning Gallagher got a call from Cohn from the airport. Soon after, Cohn was sitting across from him in his office.

"Roy, what is this that you're trying to get me involved in? The FBI is spying on the office of attorney general. Hoover is nervous about Bobby becoming president and he wants to use me to sabotage him?"

"If you do this for Mr. Hoover, he will be forever grateful. Do you know what that could mean for a man like you, Neil? What's more, Hoffa would be there for you. He'll support you in your election efforts, whatever's necessary, and the Teamsters will hire your law firm, no questions asked, for $100,000 a year."

"I didn't hear that, Roy. We're friends, but now I want you to leave this office."

"You'll be sorry, Neil Gallagher. You're going to be sorry you did this."

Gallagher walked around the desk and grabbed him by the shirt. "Are you threatening me?"

"Not me," Cohn pleaded. "But I know how they work."

"How who works?"

"The Bureau, Neil. You're either their friend or their enemy. There's no middle ground."

Gallagher let him go. "This conversation is forgotten."

"If you won't do it, there are plenty of others who will."

"Well, you just have one of them be Hoover's stooge, Roy," Gallagher said, pointing him out the door. "I won't have any part of it."

Gallagher dreaded the days that followed. Certainly, he had calculated the odds for disaster in turning down the offer, especially when only days later every detail of the contents in the suitcase was exposed, causing Kennedy much consternation and a lot of explaining. In one fell swoop, Hoover had surreptitiously leaked the material damaging to Bobby. After the affair, however, not even Gallagher, who knew and understood the unmitigated chutzpah of Cohn, could have anticipated what happened next.

He was in his office one night going through mail and signing papers when he noticed a letter addressed to Attorney General Katzenbach, already prepared and awaiting his signature:

"Dear Mr. Katzenbach, as Chairman of the Special Inquiry on Invasion of Privacy, I herewith demand that you appear before our committee and bring with you all papers and authorizations for the illegal bugging of the residences of Martin Luther King."

Gallagher never wrote such a letter. He immediately called in his secretary, Elizabeth May, and asked her about it. May said that Cohn convinced her that he had wanted the letter dictated to her so it would be ready and waiting for his signature. Gallagher thought she was joking, but May said that Cohn was very specific, asking that she get it out immediately.

On the phone, Cohn was nonchalant about the affair, which made Gallagher even angrier. Cohn said that he wasn't able to talk about it over the phone, that he'd be at his office first thing in the morning.

The next day Gallagher was still furious. "Roy, are you out of your mind? What are you trying to do, destroy me? You know, I ought to throw you out of that window. Where do you get the nerve to try to pull something like this? Are you trying ruin me? I told you, I don't want any part of this. I'm no cloak and dagger guy. I'm a legislator and, frankly, I'm still trying to figure out how the hell I got mixed up in all of this to begin with."

"It wasn't me that dictated that letter. It was Mr. Hoover. He's fed up with Bobby Kennedy passing himself off as some kind of savior to the Black race when it was he who signed the papers authorizing the bugging of King's residences all along."

"That's not my problem. Here's your letter," he said stuffing it into the front pocket of Cohn's suit jacket. "You tell Mr. Hoover that I am everybody's friend but nobody's whore. Now get the hell out of my office and don't ever show your face here again."

"Big mistake, Neil," Cohn asserted. "I'll deliver the message, but trust me, you're going to regret it."

"Is that a threat, Roy?"

"No, a warning. Be on the lookout, Neil, because they're going to get you for this."

Day by day, each piece of the puzzle began adding to the miasma of fear and distrust in Congress. Conversations, whether in corridors or offices, were anything but free and open, forcing legislators to meet with Gallagher in secret "cells" outside of conventional conference rooms that could be bugged. There they discussed how they might break loose from the choke hold of threats, blackmail and character assassination that federal law enforcement was inflicting upon the people's democratically elected leaders.

It was around this time that Gallagher saw a congressman who used to sit near him in session. He looked over to him. He was holding a brown paper bag on his lap, his face pale.

"Are you all right?" Gallagher asked. "You look like you've just seen a ghost."

He fumbled for a moment, then looked up from the filled paper bag. "I'm fine, but do you know, I've just been given this bag from Hoover," he said turning to him confidentially. "It's filled with tapes, recordings they got from microphones hidden at Ray DeCarlo's place in Mountainside."

"You're joking." Gallagher said, but then understanding just from his gaze that this was no joke.

"You know, this kind of thing could be embarrassing to someone like me because some of these Mob characters have been throwing my name around. Thank God for guys like Hoover or this could lead to some real misunderstandings."

Gallagher tried to explain. "Don't you think the FBI has copies of those tapes? Don't you see what they're really trying to tell you. Guys like that are your friends so long as you do everything they ask. But what if someday you don't feel like doing what they ask?"

He shook his head in the negative. "That's the difference between you and me, Neil. I'm not out to antagonize anyone, least of all Mr. Hoover, who, a lot of us think, does a pretty damn good job."

# THE PRIVACY WAR

## XXII
## Gallagher v. The Media

**"State police payoffs, bribery of local and state officials for the procurement of government contracts, racketeering and murder."**

If after his latest confrontation with Cohn, Gallagher was waiting for the second shoe to drop, he didn't have long.

It was noon on Tuesday, August 27, when Gallagher's daughters Patti and Bridget came home from St. Andrew's Grammar School for lunch, Rick remembers.

"Mom, is Daddy in the Mafia?" Bridget asked.

"What? Wherever did you get an idea like that? Why would you ask such a silly question?"

Bridget seemed embarrassed to answer, until finally Patti spoke up. "Because that's what the kids in her class are saying. They're saying that the newspaper says Dad's a Mafia man who steals money from people."

"Newspaper? What newspaper?" she insisted of Bridget, who seemed to know more than she was telling.

"It's not the newspaper," Bridget told Patti, holding up a copy of *Life* magazine.

It was six-page feature article titled "The Fix," outlining the basic structure of the Mafia, which included the names and photographs of prominent Mafia bosses Carlo Gambino of New York,

Sam DeCavalante of New Jersey, Meyer Lansky of Florida, Carlos Marcello of Louisiana and Sam Giancana of Illinois. Gallagher's name was also there, mentioned once. Most of the information used in the article was derived from the "Barn" tapes recorded through FBI listening devices installed in a club where Angelo DeCarlo and his buddies would meet.

[Joe] Zicarelli's domestic connections extend well beyond the confines of Hudson County, into the chambers of the U.S. Congress itself. Indeed, he is on the best of terms with the widely respected Democratic representative from Hudson County, Congressman Cornelius E. Gallagher....Bayonne Joe and his congressman seem to have a lot to talk over, judging from the frequency of their get-togethers. These usually take place far from Washington or Bayonne—where Gallagher lives and Zicarelli runs the Rackets. Sometimes the setting is a picturesque Wayside Inn off the Saw Mill River Parkway north of New York, and the occasion is an unhurried and chummy Sunday brunch.[1]

Within hours of the periodical hitting the streets, Hudson County was abuzz with rumor and speculation about Gallagher and Zicarelli.

Before going to *Life*'s offices in Manhattan, Gallagher spoke to Neil Walsh. Walsh volunteered to come along, but as they would discover, getting an audience wasn't easy. They were told that the editor was out of town, so they decided to go directly to the man in charge.

The secretary claimed he wasn't in, but Gallagher saw that the office door was closed. He walked past her and flung it open to find him sitting there.

"Who are you?" the editor demanded.

"I'm Congressman Neil Gallagher and I want to know why

you're trying to destroy my career."

"I don't know what you're talking about."

He tossed a copy of the magazine in his direction. "Well, maybe you should read the stories you print because this article about me meeting with gangsters for brunch every Sunday is an outright lie. I've never in my life been to the Wayside Inn, ever. Unless you guys want a lawsuit that will set records in this town you better print a retraction."

The editor nodded, then waved him and Walsh to follow as he took them to see another editor.

"Listen," Gallagher said. "I challenge you right now to drive me to the restaurant where your magazine says we meet and see if anyone, any person there, recognizes me as ever having set foot in the place."

The editor nodded. "Would you mind waiting outside, Congressman, while I make arrangements."

A short time later the editor walked out of his office. "We're sticking by the story and that's that," he asserted.

In newspaper articles from the New York Times to the Newark Evening News to the Jersey Journal, Gallagher took his case to the people, claiming that the article was aimed, not just at him, but at his people, the country and the president.

One week after his visit to *Life*'s offices, a second article titled "Mobsters in the Marketplace: Money, Muscle, Murder" appeared in the publication. Though Gallagher's name was not mentioned, the article reported that in the fall of 1962, the body of a Bayonne gambler was hauled by Zicarelli's men from the home of a Hudson County political figure.[2] Because of the previous *Life* article, many thought immediately of Gallagher.

Two days after the article was released, the state attorney general requested an audience with the editors of the magazine to present him with evidence in support of their accusations, which included state police payoffs, bribery of local and state officials for the procurement of government contracts, racketeering and murder. While publicly pursuing *Life*, which pledged full cooperation short of revealing its sources, the state attorney went on to request that Ramsey Clark convene a federal grand jury to investigate the magazine's charges of "widespread Cosa Nostra activity in New Jersey."[3]

Gallagher, for his part, wore the original *Life* allegations like a hair shirt. His name had been mentioned alongside Zicarelli's in newspapers across the country, but he persevered, denying any illegal involvement, slowing down only occasionally for a statement on the subject while persisting in his legislative efforts to push forward the causes associated with his unabashedly libertarian views.

The coming months were surreal for Gallagher. He remembers talking to Steve Bercik, a friend for years with whom he'd graduated law school, saying things very heartfelt and deeply personal, trying to capture the horror of what he felt was going on around him. "How would you feel," he asked Bercik, "If you woke up one morning to discover that the country you thought you'd been living in and fought for during your entire life no longer existed?" Bercik thought he was joking, but Gallagher told him that as a man who fought in two wars and served his country, he never believed he would ever lose faith in his nation.

If Gallagher had concluded anything from his political career so far, it was that a group of perhaps one hundred men were manipulating a nation of several hundred million. They were operating through blackmail, political assassination, murder and, most effectively, as he would soon see, technology.

# XXIII
## The National Data Bank Concept

**"A vast federal information file could easily be turned into an intelligence file used against millions of American citizens."**

Despite the *Life* allegations, Gallagher continued with his work. He and his subcommittee proceeded with their investigation into the National Data Bank Concept, retail credit bureaus, federal involvement in the use of behavioral modification drugs, and even the IRS. However, through a private, off-the-record meeting with a top-level behavioral psychologist from the Office of Naval Intelligence, Gallagher made a startling discovery.

An anonymous navy lieutenant assigned to a Department of Navy research facility in California came to see Gallagher on October 8, 1967. The lieutenant mentioned that he'd been reading about Gallagher's work in the field of computer science and the right of privacy. His interest stemmed from his involvement in a naval intelligence project conducted at a neuropsychiatric laboratory in San Diego where experiments were conducted to integrate human intelligence and decision-making capabilities with computers. The goal, he claimed, was to create an artificial intelligence that was capable of memory, judgment and the feeling of emotions. He claimed that this was the most terrifying experiment he'd ever heard of and that there were others that used convicted murderers from military prisons as test subjects in behavior modification experiments based on drugs, hypnosis and audio-visual desensitization.

Gallagher paused to catch his breath and explained that he didn't doubt the lieutenant's word, but still needed documentation. The lieutenant told him that if he wanted a report, he could tell him where to get one.

They agreed to meet the next evening at six o'clock in his office, but when the time came, the lieutenant was nowhere to be found. Gallagher's office checked into it and officials at the San Diego research facility told them that there was no one by the lieutenant's name working at the neuropsychiatric laboratory and that no such experiments were being, or had ever been, conducted.[1]

Interestingly, in 1991, much of what the lieutenant related to Gallagher during their bizarre 1967 encounter was corroborated. Gallagher learned that in 1972, one lieutenant commander of the U.S. Regional Medical Center in Naples, Italy, explained at an Oslo NATO conference, a researcher could find people whom they could use in experiments from the U.S. Navy. He revealed how the navy was secretly programming a large number of assassins and claimed that the men he had worked with for the navy were being prepared for covert operations in U.S. embassies worldwide. Careful screening of the subjects was accomplished by navy psychologists through military records, and those who actually received assignments were drawn mainly from submarine crews, the paratroopers and convicted murderers serving military prison sentences.

The assassins were conditioned through audio-visual desensitization, Gallagher discovered. The process involved showing films of people being injured or killed in a variety of ways, starting with mild depictions, leading up to the more extreme forms of violence. Eventually, the subjects would be able to detach their feelings even when viewing the most graphic films. The conditioning was most successful when applied to passive-aggressive types, and most of these people ended up being able to kill without regret.

During the audio-visual desensitization programming, restraints were used to force the subject to view the films. A device was used on the subject's eyelids to prevent him from blinking. Typically, the preliminary film was of an African youth being ritualistically circumcised with a dull knife and without anesthetic. The second film showed a sawmill scene in which a man accidentally cut off his fingers. In addition, the potential assassins underwent programming to create prejudicial attitudes, to think of their future enemies, especially the leaders of the countries where it had been decided they would be sent, as sub-human. Films and lectures were presented demeaning the culture and habits of the people of these countries. Ironically, the prime indicator of violent tendencies was the same personality testing that Gallagher had fought against.[2]

In a July 1968 government operations summary report, "Privacy and the National Data Bank Concept," Gallagher wrote in reaction to his findings that the subcommittee sought to "create a climate of concern" and "develop guidelines to protect privacy," but not hinder efficient operation of Government or statistical analysis in the social sciences.[3]

If a "climate of concern" was what he wanted to create, he more than succeeded as the Privacy Hearings moved on to tackle the National Data Bank Concept. The idea of a centralized government computer that could gather and forever maintain detailed personal information, including that derived from private detectives and law enforcement surveillance, was too much for Gallagher.

A vast federal information file could easily be turned into an intelligence file used against millions of American citizens. Criminal records, IRS tax returns, medical records, the results of psychological testing and data on personal and political associations could be brought together in a matter of minutes. The detailed census, long in effect before the advent of the Nazi Party, provided a most convenient tool for Hitler when he led the party to control Germany. The census information provided a central data system from which the dictator could draw detailed information on any German citizen, thereby facilitating the power surge of his totalitarian regime. It was the chief tool for tracing Jewish bloodlines in Nazi Germany.[4]

What began as an inquiry into the National Data Bank Concept became an inquiry into what kinds of supposed confidential information might become part of a government dossier on private citizens. This led to Gallagher's investigation, "The Computer and Invasion of Privacy." One retail credit company, for example, held detailed financial records on more than 45 million Americans that were routinely made available to the FBI and IRS with little or no regard for confidentiality. Commercial credit bureaus maintained files on more than 110 million citizens, issuing 97 million reports during the year 1967 alone, granting police agencies and federal investigators and even private citizens access to the files for a fee.[5]

On March 12, 1967, Alan Westin, professor of Public Law and Government, Columbia University, explained that a standard credit report might contain "items of personal identification, employment history, public records such as arrests, lawsuits, marriages, divorces, bankruptcies and credit history such as size of bank accounts, defaults and so forth. There are special credit investigations that will collect and report information about the personal character, habits, and reputation of an individual, which will be obtained by interviews with the individual's employer, his banker, his landlord, his neighbors, and fellow workers."

Westin went on to explain that the reports were generally used for credit-gaining institutions such as banks, department stores and mortgage companies. "However," Westin added, "credit files on individuals can be obtained by noncredit grantors. Police agencies and federal investigators, for example, have access to most credit bureaus. The Washington and regional offices of the Federal Bureau of Investigation are the largest users."

As an example, Westin cited a specific incident. "I asked a member of my staff at Columbia to write the executive manager of the Greater New York Credit Bureau and ask for a report on the character of a female research assistant," he explained. "He indicated that she was being considered for a promotion. At 10:00 A.M., one day later, the executive manager telephoned and read us a full 'previous residence' report on this woman containing information about her character, habits and morals, how she was regarded by her employer, whether there was any indication of illegal practices, judgments, or bankruptcies, her estimated monthly income, investments, bank accounts, and a considerable list of other items."[6]

Ultimately, revelations uncovered by the committee relating to the sharing of IRS tax returns, previously thought to be confidential, with other government agencies, congressional committees and even foreign governments, were exposed. Speaking at the American Bar Association's annual convention in Hawaii with Vice President Hubert Humphrey, with Attorney General Ramsey Clark and Chief Justice Earl Warren in attendance, Gallagher drove home his privacy theme.

Although the technology of computerization has raised new horizons of progress, it also brings with it grave dangers. The greatest of these is that we may allow ourselves to drift into a course of action that will substitute a computer for man's free will and his human consciousness of what is ethical and what is not—the computer, with its insatiable appetite for information, its image of infallibility, its inability to forget anything that has been put into it, may become the heart of a surveillance system that will turn society into a transparent world in which our home, our finances, our associations, our mental and physical condition are laid bare to the most casual observer. If information is power, then real power and its inherent threat to the Republic will rest not in some elected officials or Army generals, but in a few overzealous members of a bureaucratic elite.[7]

The speech was stirring. Shortly thereafter, prevailing on his personal relationship with Lyndon Johnson on the issue of civil liberties, he asked the president to become involved in stopping, or at least delaying, implementation of the National Data Bank Concept until concrete protections could be put in place to prevent abuse. Johnson complied, ordering Budget Bureau director Charles Schultze and his assistant, Charles Zwick, to his office the next day. In a letter Zwick wrote to Johnson, he said:

"In our study of the data center idea, we are proceeding along the line we discussed when Director Schultze and I met with you over a year ago; that is, we will prepare a specific concrete plan which could be exposed to the critical review of a group representing the broad variety of interests in the privacy matter. Only after that would we consider that we have a proposal for appropriate consideration by Congress. In view of the priorities which we must give within the total program of the Bureau, it is doubtful if we will reach this latter stage in time to make a formal presentation to this Congress.[8]

With that, the formal idea of a National Data Bank Concept was killed, earning Gallagher the undying enmity of Hoover, the CIA and U.S. Army Intelligence which, at the time according to Gallagher, had no fewer than 7,000 agents illegally spying on American citizens suspected of radical, communist or left-leaning affiliations.

Gallagher's subcommittee of three had won again, but even he had to wonder how long it could last. He wondered how much more would the leaders of government take.

A few days later, Patti Gallagher was out playing with her friends in their front yard. She came charging into their home hysterically crying that a man in a car outside their house was pointing a gun at her. Gallagher dropped everything and raced to the front door just in time to see the man sitting in an unmarked car, pointing a parabolic microphone in their direction. The man took note of him, smiled, started his engine and drove away.

## XXIV
## Hoover, King and Bobby

**"There was no grief in Hoover's office when on Wednesday, June 5, 1968, Robert Kennedy was assassinated."**

From Gallagher's side, he, too, was gearing up for a political campaign in November and though, as with Bobby Kennedy, Hoover had tried to undermine his constituency, the *Life* magazine controversy had played to the loyalty of his Hudson County supporters. They liked a good fight and could always be counted upon to rally behind the cause of an underdog. Nevertheless, Gallagher was, himself, beginning to feel disenfranchised, if not from his people, then at least from his government. He found himself wondering what kind of men these were.

It was a question that took on an entirely new meaning on the night of April 4, 1968, when Gallagher attended a Democratic fundraiser at the Statler Hilton in Washington, D.C. He was sitting at a table with Bob Burkhardt, secretary of state, along with Reverend Harold Woodson, a prominent civil rights leader, when word trickled through the crowd that Martin Luther King had been assassinated. A terrible sigh went up from the crowd. People started to scream. But as the total disbelief and sadness settled, and the dinner disintegrated as people began to leave, Reverend Woodson began to sob. "What are they doing to my people?" he cried. "What are they doing to my America?" King's assassination would spark riots in cities throughout the United States. The FBI responded by escalating its harassment campaign, this time against King's widow, Coretta Scott King.

In late 1975, the Church Committee hearings on King's assassination learned of a nine-hour meeting among the FBI's elite to figure out how to spy upon and intimidate King. Later, two Atlanta agents met with the FBI to decide "how best to carry on our investigation to produce the desired results without embarrassment to the Bureau."[1]

Through a combination of premonition and knowledge, Gallagher came to understand what had truly happened to his friend. Since 1964 the challenge had been to trigger enough despair in King for him to back down. They sent him death threats and anonymously mailed copies of tapes and sexually explicit photos to Coretta Scott King at their home in Atlanta.

> King, In view of your low grade {censored by FBI} I will not dignify your name with either a Mr. or a Reverend or a Dr. . . . Look into your heart. You know you are a complete fraud and a great liability to all of us Negroes . . . You are no clergyman and you know it. You are a colossal fraud and an evil, vicious one at that....You could have been our greatest leader. Your "honorary" degrees, your Nobel Prize and other awards will not save you. King, I repeat, you are done. King, there is only one thing left for you to do. You know what it is. You have just 34 days in which to do [it]. You are done. There is but one way out for you. You better take it before your filthy, abnormal fraudulent self is bared to the nation.[2]

The same was happening to him, Gallagher suspected. Both he and King were deemed suitable targets for COINTELPRO.

Gallagher was suitable for the work his subcommittee was doing and for his refusal to cooperate with Hoover's planned destruction of Bobby Kennedy. King was suitable because Hoover, Gallagher believes, genuinely despised and feared him, believing he was a communist and the potential catalyst for a future race war.

So depressed that he couldn't eat or sleep, King was overheard through an FBI listening device saying, "They are out to break me." As if proud to have brought on King's emotional crisis, Hoover sent a report citing the remark and other indications of personal distress to the White House. But the callousness and harassment didn't end there. When the news that King was shot in Memphis came over the radio, shouts saying "They got Zorro! They finally got the son a bitch!" echoed through the corridors of the FBI office. When word came a short time later that he was dead, one agent literally jumped for joy. [3]

And, of course, there was Bobby Kennedy. A major source of friction during Bobby's days as attorney general was the department's primary mission. To Hoover, it had always been and would remain domestic Communism. To Kennedy, who was convinced the director was himself being blackmailed by the Mafia over his homosexual relationships, it was organized crime.

Bobby Kennedy entered the Justice Department with a hit list, and Hoover and Hoffa were on it. But Hoover had a hate list, the anecdote goes, where Martin Luther King and Bobby Kennedy shared top billing. Once Gallagher refused to use his Privacy Hearings as a weapon to settle Hoover's vendetta with Bobby, the director used Cohn as a go-between to supply information damaging to the attorney general to a Hoffa intimate.

After years of trying to convict the Union leader of virtually any crime possible, Hoffa was convicted of jury tampering and sentenced to eight years in federal prison. A Hoffa intimate summarized the government misconduct that formed the basis of a raft of subsequent appeals, saying that they uncovered surveillance of their attorneys, illegal wiretapping of their phones and the bugging of their conference rooms. They even brought forth documented evidence that U.S. marshals mishandled the jury. They had proof that the marshals were wiretapping the jury deliberations as well as affidavits and sworn testimonies that the same marshals furnished alcoholic beverages and prostitutes to the jurors.[4]

And there was no grief in Hoover's office when on Wednesday, June 5, 1968, Robert Kennedy was assassinated in the kitchen of the Ambassador Hotel in Los Angeles.

# XXV
# Programming the Assassins

**" ...cogs in a single, stupendous murder machine."**

From the National Data Bank Concept, Gallagher's Committee moved to the issue of the upcoming census. "The census is the best source of information about the voter and its unchecked use could threaten the free election process," he cautioned. "As this information becomes more and more valuable to would-be political leaders, the conditions for political blackmail becomes increasingly ripe."[1]

The supposition led shortly thereafter to hearings on the subject that uncovered the fact that the original National Data Bank Concept, far from disappearing, had simply permutated. Gallagher feels that the Bureau of Census had simply been substituted as the procurer of personal data for the Bureau of Statistics, which was to have originally performed this service for the U.S. Army and FBI. In hearings held before the Committee, Gallagher's testimony led to the revelation that confidential census information was not only shared with agencies such as the IRS and FBI, but was also being sold wholesale to commercial companies for the creation of mailing lists.

But the heart of the issue went far beyond mailing lists. Since Hoover had created dossiers on nearly every influential representative in the United States Congress, the creation of a centralized data base that included IRS returns, personality test results, credit reports, medical records, police files and more, Gallagher now asks, which American citizen would not be vulnerable to federal law enforcement investigation and coercion?

In testimony given to Rep. Paul Krebs on the subject of census questions and their presumed confidentiality, Gallagher made no pretense at disguising what he believed to be the issue at hand:

> It doesn't take much to convert a democracy into something else. For centuries, European nations innocently collected detailed information about their citizens through censuses and later through identification cards or passports. The use of such information was never conceived of for reasons other than efficiency and economy. We should not forget that it was just such a system that facilitated the mass murders in Germany during the late thirties and forties. On the basis of what we can learn from the utilization of the frage-bogen in Nazi Germany, we should be able to recognize all of the practices to which centralized data can be put to use.
>
> I refer to my statement about the fragebogen, a questionnaire established under Hitler in the towns and villages that helped him centralize information into a central data bank. This was done without a computer. Today, if you put all of this information into a central data bank, you would have a dossier on each American citizen existing at the other end of a button which would yield instantaneous retrieval of more than just information, but a kind of profile whose use would rely almost entirely upon the good will and trust of the person who retrieved it.[2]

It was one thing to be nosing around programs peripheral to the major thrusts of the FBI, CIA, Department of Defense and others, but in those early days of 1968, Gallagher's Subcommittee on

Privacy was getting dangerously close to the "family jewels" as they were known in intelligence circles: hundreds of millions of dollars spent annually on the mastery of lethal nerve gasses such as BZ and VX; the creation of deadly biological weapons such as anthrax, tularemia and Q fever; and the latest concept, using gene splicing to produce an ethnic chemical weapon, designed to target specific population groups.[3]

All of this was devastatingly significant, but, at the time, not nearly as important as the information Gallagher's Privacy Hearings were uncovering on experiments in behavioral modification on unsuspecting American adults and, more specific, American children.

The first experiment Gallagher discovered was the unauthorized dispensing of psychotic drugs including Ritalin, Dexedrine and Melleril to 250,000 grammar school children. The second was a federally funded study undertaken in Maryland where thousands of boys between the ages of six and eight were required to give blood in an attempt to determine which of them had an anomalous extra Y chromosome, which was linked to antisocial behavior. The third was a proposal for nationwide psychological testing to identify students who had a propensity toward criminal behavior for isolation in "youth camps" where their personalities could be altered through behavioral modification techniques. The fourth was the chilling revelation to Gallagher that Harvard professor B. F. Skinner's landmark work on the subject, *Beyond Freedom and Dignity* had been funded by a U.S. government grant.[4]

There was more to the story when Gallagher considered these drugs in relation to the assassinations of the Kennedys and King. First, their proximity in time; second, the fact that each of the victims was considered a mortal enemy of both the FBI and the CIA; third, the assassination of foreign leaders, euphemistically referred to as "wet jobs," had been exercised by the CIA as a matter of policy since its inception; fourth, there is today ample evidence that hundreds of millions of dollars and no fewer than thirteen years of experimentation prior to Bobby Kennedy's assassination had been devoted to the science of mind control and, more specific, the creation of programmed assassins.

Given this final point and the fact that ultimately it was the subject of behavioral modification that Gallagher's Privacy Subcommittee was headed toward in 1968, it seemed appropriate to him to examine not the victims or the institutions, for means and motive were established, but rather the assassins themselves. Their personalities, backgrounds and the observations made by others about them were all of interest to Gallagher. It was a mix, both odd and compelling, that may lead one to conclude that the reason for Gallagher's downfall had little to do with the Mafia and everything to do with his subcommittee's inquiries and the powerful enemies those hearings had earned him.

In one of the more surreal moments in television history, Truman Capote, author of *In Cold Blood*, espoused a theory on Johnny Carson's *Tonight Show* while James Earl Ray, King's assassin, was still at large, which so captivated the late-night host that he canceled all scheduled guests for the evening. He told Carson that he had studied the record carefully and that James Earl Ray was simply not capable of such a cruel and calculated crime. "In my opinion, Ray, as well as Lee Harvey Oswald in Dallas and Sirhan Sirhan in Los Angeles, are all cogs in a single, stupendous murder machine," Capote postulated.

Beyond Capote's conjecture, Gallagher believes there was much to link Ray; Oswald; Bobby Kennedy's assassin, Sirhan Sirhan; and even Jack Ruby, some of it obvious, much of it bizarre. Beginning with the obvious, each of the assassins had near-perfect backgrounds for the job: Ray, the Southern racist; Oswald, the Marxist; Sirhan, the Arab terrorist; Ruby, the Mafia hoodlum. They were all so easy to hate at first sight. But James Earl Ray was a totally non-political and non-assertive man. "He's definitely not like any Negro-killer I've ever known," reported Arthur Hanes, Ray's attorney and former FBI agent. "I don't think he hates Negroes. I don't think he has strong feelings about anything."[5]

In the case of Oswald, "there was no evidence of particular animus by Oswald toward Kennedy," wrote Norman Mailer in *Oswald's Tale*. "And more than a few key witnesses testified [before the Warren Commission] to Oswald's positive utterances concerning JFK."[6] Jack Ruby, ostensibly killed Oswald to "spare Mrs. Kennedy the pain of a trial," but rarely spoke of Oswald and, in fact, later wrote, "I was used to silence Oswald . . . they found some very clever ways to trick me."[7] Finally, in an interview with attorney Grant Cooper, Sirhan, whose motive was supposed to be political, stated, "I honestly did not decide to do it, sir. Objectively, I had no awareness of what I was doing that night."[8]

Gallagher believes that a second commonality was the blatant evidence each man left behind, for in the case of Oswald, Ruby, Sirhan and certainly Ray, who fled the country, it was impossible to be any more self-incriminating. Oswald left behind his mail-ordered Mannlicher-Carcano rifle in the book depository, covered with fingerprints, surrounded by neatly aligned expended shells. He had asked his wife to take the now-famous photograph of him holding the weapon three weeks before.

In Ruby's case, he rushed into a crowded tunnel leading out of the Dallas detention center, killed Oswald, then charged into the arms of the police and detectives gathered for the assassin's transfer.

Then there is Ray, a man with a level of sophistication that allowed him to gain fraudulent passports for use in the United

States, Mexico, Canada and England. He allegedly shot King, then ran to his white Mustang convertible, dropping his Remington rifle with his fingerprints on it onto the street in a Browning box that could be traced to the store where it was purchased.

Again, if there were to remain any doubt about his involvement, he left behind a zippered bag that contained underwear with traceable laundry marks and a transistor radio with his Jefferson City prison ID number.

The blatant evidence in Sirhan's case amounted to roughly the same as Ruby's with one notable exception: On the desktop of the rooming house where he resided, Sirhan left a diary with the phrase "Robert Kennedy must be assassinated," handwritten fourteen times on the final page.[9]

More bizarre to Gallagher however was the foundation upon which the personalities of each of these men were based, their undeniable exposure to hypnosis and the ambiguity surrounding the crimes themselves. The personality of Oswald, the would-be revolutionary, marine and intellectual, is precisely captured in *Oswald's Tale* when Mailer states that "Lee was a man with many compartments in his life."

Jack Ruby, police groupie and small-time hoodlum with powerful Mafia friends, was diagnosed by Dr. Roy Schafer, professor of Psychiatry at Yale, as "dissociated . . . not altogether in control of his body actions as if they occur independently of his conscious will at times."[10]

The personality of James Earl Ray was determined to be "passive-aggressive," as his attorney, Arthur Hanes, explained. "He is well informed, but his views are neither extreme nor bitterly held. I never heard him express or saw him display resentment, hatred or malice toward anyone. The psychiatrists in Missouri who examined Ray told me: 'From what we know of him it's hard for us to believe he was capable of the initiative required to commit such a crime.'"[11]

The situation with Sirhan Sirhan was even more marked as clinical psychologist Dr. Martin Schorr testified that Sirhan was in a "dissociate state at the time of the murder." "Dis-associate?" asked Judge Walker, who presided over the case. "Dissociate," Schorr answered. "A personality structure that was in a high degree of fragmentation."[12]

Beyond this, each one of the four assassins had had deep and demonstrable exposure to sophisticated levels of behavior-altering hypnosis prior to their apprehension by authorities.

The following exchange between Attorney Mark Jenner and Oswald's brother, Robert, was taken from Warren Commission testimony:

> JENNER: Having in mind the changes in physical appearance . . . have you formed an opinion, Mr. Oswald, as to whether your brother may have undergone some treatment of some kind in Russia that affected his mind?

> ROBERT OSWALD: Yes, sir. Since Lee's death on November 24th, I have formed an opinion in that respect.

> JENNER: What is that opinion?

> ROBERT OSWALD: . . . perhaps something in the nature of shock treatments or something along that line had been given to him in Russia . . . when he came back, he had the deadest eyes I ever saw.[13]

The tie to hypnosis with James Earl Ray is less defined, Gallagher believes, but equally compelling. FBI records tell us that on January 4, 1968, exactly four months before he allegedly killed King, Ray kept an appointment he had made with the director of the International Society of Hypnosis, the Reverend Xavier von Koss, at his office in the South Bay area of Los Angeles. Von Koss specialized in self-improvement seminars and described himself as an internationally recognized authority on hypnosis. When questioned about his work with Ray and, specifically, if he had hypnotized him, von Koss said, "I tested him for hypnosis, but quickly encountered very strong subconscious resistance so I didn't press any further. I could do nothing but recommend a few books for him to study: *Self Hypnotism: The Technique and Its Use in Daily Living* by Leslie M. LeCron and *Psycho-Cybernetics* by Maxwell Maltz."[14]

When Ray was arrested at a London airport while using the alias George Sneyd, he had in his possession a pistol, two passports, a birth certificate, a Polaroid camera, a radio, the 1967 almanac and three books on self-hypnosis.

Since extensive psychiatric study was done on Ruby following his murder of Oswald, there was much to link him to hypnosis and the behavior-modification techniques he had apparently undergone. Dr. Manfred S. Guttmacher, chief medical officer of the Supreme Court of Baltimore and a leading expert on criminal psychology, testified that Ruby's brain had been damaged and that he felt Ruby at the time of the shooting suffered a functional psychosis. When Assistant District Attorney Bill Alexander asked what he meant by functional mental psychosis, Guttmacher said a psychotic condition for which there was no organic cause. Alexander protested that on the one hand, Guttmacher was saying Ruby had brain damage, but on the other hand he was saying, no, he did not have brain damage. But the confusion was real for, more to the point, Ruby's brain had not been damaged, but tampered with, a concept better expressed in later testimony by Dr.

Walter Bromberg, clinical director of Pinewood Psychiatric Hospital. "Jack Ruby was pre-set to be a fighter, to attack. Definitely there is a block to his thinking which is no part of his original mental endowment."

Easily the strongest evidence for hypnotic programming, Gallagher believes, was the situation of Sirhan Sirhan. The three prescribed building blocks of MKULTRA were: 1) to induce hypnosis very rapidly in unwitting subjects, 2) to create durable amnesia and 3) to implant durable and operationally useful posthypnotic suggestion. Gallagher contrasted this to the court testimony of Dr. Bernard Diamond, professor of Psychiatry at the University of California, in which he said that it was immediately apparent that Sirhan had been programmed because his response to hypnosis was strange in that he exhibited a phenomenon of automatic writing, which is something that can only be done when one is pretty well trained. Once he was finally hypnotized and asked about the notebooks in his room, the following exchange between he and his examiner occurred:

> "Is this crazy writing?"
>
> "Yes, yes, yes, yes, yes, yes, yes."
>
> "Are you crazy?"
>
> "No, no, no, no."
>
> "Why are you writing crazy?"
>
> "Practice, practice, practice, practice, practice."
>
> "Practice for what?"
>
> "Mind control, mind control, mind control, mind control."
>
> "Who wrote your notebooks?"
>
> "I, I, I, I, I, I."
>
> "Were you hypnotized when you wrote the notebook?"

"Yes, yes, yes."

"Who hypnotized you when you wrote the notebook?"

"Mirror, mirror, my mirror, my mirror, my mirror, my mirror, my mirror, my mirror."[15]

The MKULTRA skeptic admits that none of the arguments he uses against a conditioned assassin would apply to a programmed patsy whom a hypnotist could walk through a series of seemingly unrelated events: a visit to a store, a conversation with a mailman, picking a fight at a political rally. The subject would remember everything that happened to him and be amnesic only for the fact that the hypnotist ordered him to do these things. There would be no gaping inconsistencies in his life of the sort that could ruin an attempt by a hypnotist to create a second personality.

The purpose of this exercise, Gallagher believes, was to leave a circumstantial trail that would make the authorities think the patsy committed a particular crime. Gallagher argues that the weakness might well have been that amnesia would not hold up under police interrogation, but that would not matter if the police did not believe his preposterous story about being hypnotized or if he were shot resisting arrest. Hypnosis expert Milton Kline said he could create a patsy in three months; an assassin would take him six.[16]

Who is to say that behavioral modification was not a key element in the orchestration of these assassinations, Gallagher asks today. It had been used overseas in Operation Phoenix to create programmed killers with great effect. More, even a cursory look at the circumstances surrounding these individuals demonstrates a degree of coincidence that boggles the imagination. Both Oswald and Ray, supposedly penniless, began purchasing hundreds of dollars worth of sophisticated camera and radio equipment prior to the assassinations. In the case of Sirhan, who spoke incessantly about mirrors and shiny lights, his own government-appointed psychiatrist theorized that he'd undergone some type of self-hypnosis prior to shooting Bobby Kennedy.

Even Ruby obsessed about the phone call he received from Little Lyn, one of his strippers, moments before putting a bullet into Oswald. Prolonged hospital stays, hypnosis, radios, shining lights and sophisticated camera equipment were all elements that appeared over and over in the backgrounds of each of these men.

With Gallagher's subcommittee on Privacy on the verge of uncovering behavioral-modification experiments on military personnel and unsuspecting American citizens, there could be no secret more explosive or damning to the government, as Gallagher soon learned.

# XXVI
## Persecution Turns to Prosecution

### "The whole O'Brien thing is part of an FBI frame-up designed against Gallagher"

On July 3, 1968, less than one month after the RFK assassination, editors from *Life* magazine came to visit Gallagher's Washington, D.C., office after he'd agreed to discuss another exposé involving information allegedly gathered by the publication. It was then that he attempted to defend himself against, perhaps, the most outrageous allegations ever leveled against a representative of the United States Congress.

After eight months of investigations, *Life*, according to Gallagher, claimed it finally had concrete evidence against him from electronic surveillance of Zicarelli's favorite bar in Manhattan, his home and a nearby payphone.

"Maybe it's time to put your cards on the table, gentlemen," attorney Larry Weisman chimed in. "What's this harassment really about?"

They wanted an opportunity for Gallagher to answer the charges they were going to be making in an article titled "The Congressman and the Hoodlum" three weeks from then.

"When did you meet Harold Konigsberg?" they asked. Konigsberg, a local hoodlum, had been talking about Gallagher.

Not long before, he told the FBI about a dozen bodies in a pit on a farm in Lakewood, New Jersey. A Cosa Nostra "cemetery" he called it. When Konigsberg took the FBI over there, they found an orthopedic shoe. The shoe belonged to a local named Barney O'Brien.

"Harold Konigsberg has testified that Barney O'Brien's body was removed from the basement of your home on the night of October 14, 1962."

"That's the most bizarre story I've ever heard," Gallagher cried.

"He testified that O'Brien died in your house and that you dragged the body down into the basement."

"*Life* is supposed to be a reputable magazine. Do you guys have any regard for the truth at all?"

"Did O'Brien die in your house?"

"I don't know where the hell O'Brien died or even if he died or anything about him other than what appeared in the papers. Barney O'Brien was never in my house, and I categorically deny anything even vaguely resembling what you've just stated here today."

They then asked Gallagher to take a lie-detector test to prove that he wasn't a collaborator of the Cosa Nostra as Konigsberg and FBI electronic surveillance had established, but Gallagher refused. Anyone who read the papers knew that he had had his battle with lie-detector tests in the past.

The days between Gallagher's meeting *Life* and the publication of the article were filled with a donnybrook of charges, threats and countercharges. On August 2, 1968, the Newark *Star-Ledger* reported that Konigsberg planned to sue *Life* for $100,000 if it didn't pull the article.[1]

Regardless of the allegations, Gallagher garnered support from other quarters, some predictable, others downright strange, as was the unlikely help he received from Konigsberg, who simply refused to see him become the victim of a law enforcement frame. In a statement through his attorney, Konigsberg said that Gallagher never had anything to do with a dead body in his basement.[2]

Then on August 7, the *Hudson Dispatch* reported that Jeremiah J. O'Callaghan, an independent candidate seeking Gallagher's congressional seat, had sent a telegram to Vice President Hubert Humphrey and John Kenny demanding that Gallagher be dropped from the November ticket. Gallagher had outlived his usefulness, according to O'Callaghan. Kenny would not comment on the congressman's problems, but the State Democratic Committee was already researching the law on a replacement and Humphrey had joined in the call for the congressman's resignation.

The following day, Rep. Chuck Joelson publicly demanded details on the supposed wiretaps leaked by the FBI to *Life* magazine, which were used to write the story. On August 8 Joelson announced that he wrote a letter to Attorney General Ramsey Clark requesting information about whether the alleged electronic surveillance involving Gallagher was conducted by the Justice Department, and if so how that information wound up in the hands of reporters. He claimed he wrote the letter to inquire about two things: whether the Justice Department engaged in unlawful wiretapping and whether it leaked information to reporters. Fully aware that this exposure could make him a target for surveillance, he proceeded, claiming that unless someone spoke out, American democracy would go down the road to a Big Brother state.[3]

On August 9, 1968, the six-page article linking Gallagher with Konigsberg and O'Brien hit newsstands nationwide. Upon the article's release Gallagher received a telephone call from attorney Larry Weisman. He was calling on behalf of Cohn. "He knows you're pissed off at him," Weisman said. "But this *Life* thing runs deeper than you think and he wants you to know all that's involved."

Calculating the advantage of information against the disadvantage of exposure to even more of the misery Cohn had brought him, Gallagher opted to meet them at Newark Airport the following day.

Neil Walsh accompanied Weisman but left as Gallagher and Weisman walked to a remote area.

"Roy feels terrible about what's happening," Weisman began. "He tried to warn you, Neil, but you can be a stubborn guy. Now they want only one thing: your resignation."

"Who is 'they,' Larry?"

"Mr. Hoover, others."

"What others?"

"The people at *Life* for starters. You've really managed to piss them off and they've got more on you than you realize."

"More what?"

"Information, stuff they didn't use in the article that was held back in the interest of discretion."

"Discretion? They have done everything in their power to crucify me. Tell me exactly what information you're referring to."

"Cohn says they've got proof Rick's been running around on you, Neil, that Barney O'Brien not only died in your house, but in your bed. They say they have proof that Barney had a heart attack making love to your wife and will use it if you don't step down from Congress in the next ten days."

Weisman's words were like a knee to the groin.

"Do you believe that, Larry?"

"It doesn't matter what I believe. They're going to print it if you don't resign." Weisman turned to leave, but Gallagher grabbed his arm.

"Larry, do you know that FBI agents broke into an apartment that my daughter and her three girlfriends had taken for the summer in Washington? College kids. They wanted to know which of the 'broads' I was sleeping with. So listen now and deliver this message to Hoover. I'm not resigning."

That night Gallagher sat at the dinner table after the girls had gone to bed staring at the magazine, reading the words over and over again as if somehow they would change before his eyes. When he closed his eyes he could still see the words as if they were tattooed on the backs of his eyelids. Rick then came to sit with him and Gallagher told her the story.

"What kind of monsters are these?" she cried.

"These are evil men who will lie about anyone and will do absolutely anything to have their way."

They spent the entire night discussing alternatives until finally Gallagher realized that it simply wasn't in either him or Rick to quit, no matter how tough the situation got, no matter what the agencies did to them. More, it made them wonder how many civilians were threatened or intimidated in the same way.

The days that followed the distribution of the article were a roller-coaster ride of emotions for Gallagher. But still, there were encouraging signs. During an August 18, 1968, prison interview with Hudson County prosecutor, James Tumulty, Konigsberg stated under oath, "The whole O'Brien thing is part of an FBI frame-up designed against Gallagher."[4] Later that month, the connection was made: October 14, 1962 was the evening on which Gallagher was in attendance at the party in celebration of Jimmy Fair's acquittal.

# THE PRIVACY WAR

## XXVII
## Fighting to Regain his Political Career

**"Top New Jersey Democrats were about to formally request that he not attend the National Democratic Convention."**

Gallagher emerged from the second week of August 1968 politically wounded, but not yet dead. Despite the pessimism about his political future, he understood that the support he enjoyed among his constituency would work for him in the end.

Of course, time was of the essence, but if he could tap into that unique culture of loyalty he'd seen displayed in the past for men like Frank Hague and John Kenny in Hudson County, the tide could be turned at a grassroots level. He needed an occasion, however, and the opportunity presented itself on August 13, 1968, while making his first public appearance since the *Life* article at a Polish American political rally in Bayonne.

It was billed as a non-partisan event, but by the time he arrived, thirty carloads of banner-waiving supporters were waiting for him outside the union hall with another seven hundred inside. People wanted to be there for him, as they perceived he had been there for them all along. The speech was a good one. He reminded his followers who he was, where he'd come from and how he'd come to be their representative while giving them some of the background to the recent allegations. So it came as a shock just one day later when Gallagher learned that top New Jersey Democrats were about to formally request that he not attend the National Democratic Convention to be held on August 24. They did not want the attention of the controversy surrounding Gallagher.

Gallagher's strategy to hold onto his base of grassroots support while seeking to reclaim his reputation was multifold. First, he demanded that Hudson County Prosecutor Tumulty convene a grand jury for an investigation of the *Life* charges. Second, he petitioned the House Standards Committee to investigate and report on the allegations leveled against him. Finally, he began his own probe of J. Edgar Hoover.

Of course, Hoover had become a living icon to millions. He had skillfully cast himself as a hero who had created the FBI. He was the nemesis of bandits such as Machine Gun Kelly, Baby Face Nelson, Alvin "Creepy" Karpis and, of course, the brash Midwest outlaw, John Dillinger. President Harry Truman had awarded him the Medal for Merit for outstanding service to the United States. He was also the man whom President Dwight Eisenhower chose as the first-ever recipient of the Award for Distinguished Federal Civilian Service, and whom President Franklin Roosevelt charged with protecting the internal security of the United States, combating Nazis, communists, and all others who might seek to undermine the nation's security.

But Gallagher was finally convinced by now that Hoover had set out to destroy his political career. Through his probe, Gallagher began to understand what he imagined were the ordeals of Martin Luther King, Hale Boggs, Senator Joseph Tydings and John McCormack. He learned of the wiretapping of congressional offices and the illegal use of IRS, census and U.S. Army computerized records and compiled a fifteen-page statement that he promised to read before Congress at noon every day the House of Representatives was in session until J. Edgar Hoover was impeached.

> Mr. Speaker, this is corruption at the highest levels of government, and its central figure is J. Edgar Hoover. It is he whose unchecked reign of absolute power has intimidated this Congress to the extent that a serious question has not been asked about his management of the Federal Bureau of Investigation for 10 years—maybe longer. My quarrel is not with the brave men who risk their lives now as in the past to combat terrorists, murderers and those who owe allegiance to a foreign enemy. No, Mr. Speaker, my quarrel is with the political arm of the FBI that regards the decent American as the enemy. I am talking about the FBI which intimidates Congress and dares Presidents to try to control it—the FBI which employs informers, spies, and an array of sophisticated surveillance devices, not to pursue enemies of the United States but to destroy citizens of the United States.
>
> I am talking about a Federal police force who through grants, compatible computerized information systems, and often sheer brute force and fear is making every local police force totally dependent on Federal good will and financing, about a surveillance subculture and police state mentality which has set loose an investigative insanity that threatens the ability of every elected official—National, State and local—to properly function. . . . Mr. Speaker, J. Edgar Hoover should resign. If he will not, he should be fired.[1]

Shortly thereafter, Gallagher visited Cohn at his law office and handed him a piece of paper. Cohn thought it was Gallagher's resignation and said that he was doing the right thing, but soon realized it was a typewritten letter listing Hoover's misconducts. "Most of it is common knowledge around Washington," Gallagher said. "The rest I made up, just like they're making stuff about me and my wife."

Gallagher continued to explain that he had an additional paragraph saying that he would ask Cohn to confirm or deny the allegations made against him. He demanded that he would tolerate no more unfounded allegations and that no one would scare him out of office. But despite their falling out, he and Cohn met the following day at the 21 Club in Manhattan.

"Mr. Hoover doesn't know why you're mad at him," Cohn explained. "And he wants you to know he's not your enemy. What do you want him to do?"

He demanded that Hoover retract the transcript that he believed Hoover turned over to *Life* magazine. Cohn said he'd see what he could do.

On August 14, 1968, Attorney General Ramsey Clark called a press conference to publicly respond to Chuck Joelson's inquiry concerning the transcripts claiming that the FBI did not and never had any transcripts that could be the basis for the quotations in the *Life* magazine story. He added that the Justice Department was investigating all federal agencies that might have been involved in wiretapping.[2]

This was the sign Gallagher wanted. He believed the FBI had either been caught, having to admit illegal wiretapping and leaking the information to *Life* or, more to his point, Gallagher believed *Life* had been set up by Hoover with a fabricated story and was now left twisting in the wind with Clark's official denial. But he still worried that even this would be enough to exonerate him. Through hard experience he'd learned that once public persecutions began they had a way of taking on a life of their own. So he decided to proactively handle what actually had happened by going public with the truth behind the story.

He prepared a statement on the subjects of Zicarelli, the State Department and his involvement with covert foreign policy. At a press conference in the House Caucus Room on August 15, Gallagher explained his association with Zicarelli and the Cuban Missile Crisis. But the second element of his relationship with Zicarelli that revolved around Joaquin Balaguer remained a matter of national security. This coming on the heels of now-known CIA covert action regarding the assassination of Juan Bosch's predecessor Rafael Trujillo in 1961 would have produced a firestorm of criticism and undermined State Department initiatives in Latin America for decades to come. Gallagher remained quiet on the subject though officials at the highest levels issued official statements refuting *Life*'s allegations declaring his visits to that country always official. [3]

Still, the controversy continued as John Kenny finally threw his formidable support behind Gallagher's candidacy for re-election against Republican challenger Marion Dwyer. On the very same day, August 30, *Life* denounced Attorney General Ramsey Clark's former statements regarding Gallagher and the wiretap transcripts.

> *Life* stands by its story, and adds the following: Nearly a year ago, after *Life* had first described the acquaintanceship between the "Congressman and the Hoodlum," a federal law-enforcement agency reported the following to Attorney General Clark, himself: During the course of the FBI's investigation of Joseph Zicarelli, a notorious La Cosa Nostra hoodlum, confidential sources have advised on numerous occasions that Rep. Gallagher is a close friend of Zicarelli. Reliable sources have reported that Zicarelli has been in frequent contact with Gallagher and has sought the latter's favorable intervention with law enforcement authorities in the Bayonne,

N.J., area who were interfering with gambling operations conducted within Zicarelli's group.

Finally, Attorney General Clark also has been told that the Department of Justice is in possession of information received from microphone sources—which definitely reflect conversations between Zicarelli and Gallagher—indicating unquestionably that Gallagher was aiding Zicarelli's gambling interests.[4]

In a stinging reply to the magazine's editors, published in *Life*'s next issue under the title, "A Letter from the Attorney General," Clark fired back.

The accusatory power of the Department of Justice must never be used openly or covertly, merely to inform the public or defame any person. To do so would change not only the nature of the Department, but of our nation as well. No such action shall ever be permitted while I am Attorney General. Anyone violating this principle will be subject to stern disciplinary action. If *Life* magazine disagrees with this principle, we disagree.

In essence, I was asked whether I had checked into reports that the source of the *Life* article the "Congressman and the Hoodlum" was conversation overheard by the FBI using electronic surveillance. I replied that no divulgence would ever be authorized and that the FBI advises me that the quotes in *Life* do not appear in any FBI surveillance logs and could not have emanated from the FBI.

Speaking for myself, I can assure you that the Department would not hesitate to investigate or prosecute a congressman or a hoodlum if the evidence warranted federal action. Any inference to the contrary is a disservice to the rule of law, to the Department and to its personnel.[5]

Clark made two important points according to Gallagher. First, he addressed the conversations that provided the basis for the *Life* article in question. Second, he made a specific point regarding the fact that if other taped conversations of Zicarelli and Gallagher existed, they did not constitute evidence that would warrant federal action. In other words, freedom from association still existed in the United States, and an individual's mere proximity to someone who was reputed to be a criminal was deemed circumstantial.

As Gallagher moved on to the Democratic National Convention in Chicago still reeling from the previous several months, a panorama of violence rose. Nineteen sixty-eight was marked by chaos. There was the assassination of Robert Kennedy and the Tet Offensive, which severely damaged Johnson's credibility. More than 100,000 demonstrators, led by the Youth International Party, converged in Chicago decrying the Vietnam War and racism. In music, an anthem to psychedelic surrealism, *Sergeant Pepper's Lonely Hearts Club Band* topped the pop charts as the Beatles themselves paid homage to the Maharishi Maresh Yogi in India.

The literature of the day conveyed equal disdain for Western convention. Tom Wolfe's bestseller *The Electric Kool-Aid Acid Test* documented the road adventures of novelist Ken Kessey and his band of Hippies, the Merry Pranksters, leading the way for authors like Hunter S. Thompson to shed the constraints of conventional reporting for New Journalism.

Inside the convention center in Chicago, a local businessman named John LeFante presented Gallagher and the New Jersey delegation with a signed petition of over 15,000 signatures urging him to stay in the race. John McCormack made his way over to shake Gallagher's hand. But popular support among his constituents would not be a sanctuary from attacks, which Gallagher discovered on October 21 when *Life* published yet another article, this one titled "The Congressman and the Salad Oil Swindler." The article contained photos of Gallagher and a solitary shot of a Bayonne businessman, who, five years earlier, was sentenced to seven years in prison for embezzlement after his vegetable oil company went bankrupt.[6]

Gallagher's law firm unsuccessfully represented the businessman, whose associates formed a similar business, securing loans totaling $300,000 one year later through the bank where Gallagher was a director. Knowing both founders, Gallagher co-signed as guarantor of the loan based on bank approved collateral. The money was paid back to the bank in full within the year.

Charges followed in the campaign as both of Gallagher's opponents, Republican Marion Dwyer and Independent Jeremiah O'Callahan hammered away at his alleged ties to the Mafia. With a House Ethics Committee probe underway and a Hudson County grand jury convening to further study *Life* magazine's claims, Gallagher, needless to say, was an easy target.

Despite the controversy, Gallagher's friends and neighbors did not surrender their support. They felt that their congressman understood Hudson County, the haven for immigrants and blue collar workers, better than anyone. They had pride in their heritage and their work. And their support paid off. On November 4, 1968, Gallagher claimed victory over Dwyer and O'Callahan by a margin of nearly two-to-one and six-to-one respectively with 30,000 votes more than Dwyer, his nearest competitor.

# XXVIII
# The Huston Plan

**"Everything is valid, everything is possible."**

On the evening of December 14, 1968, Gallagher's "kitchen cabinet" of advisers gathered in preparation for a post-campaign rally at the Elks Club in Bayonne. The family had just finished dinner and there was a feeling of relief and triumph at having come through November's election. Gallagher wondered how much strength he had. Between the grand jury inquiry and the Ethics Committee investigation, he seemed to be perpetually waiting.

Five hundred people were reported to have shown up. John Kenny and Bayonne mayor Francis Fitzpatrick were among the speakers who stood by Gallagher's side with Kenny saying that Gallagher was one of the finest public officials in the United States and that he supported him 100 percent.[1]

As they marched forward in a phalanx of support, reporters swarmed Gallagher as he took the podium. "Tonight I pledge to you two more years of legislative action, not slander, of facts, not fiction, and of discussion, not dictation," he began. "The people of this district have given me all the strength I need to stand up and fight a mammoth publishing empire that has sought to destroy not only me, but also the principles for which we all stand. The strength of America lies in the basic decency of our people. This strength exists despite the attempts of certain elements in our society to dictate who shall be in public office and what these officeholders shall do."

During the course of that year and the next, Gallagher, living up to his word, introduced and saw the House pass the Gun Control Act; the Veterans in Public Service Act; the Occupational Safety Act; which set the groundwork for the Occupational Safety and Health Administration and assured workers minimum safety and health standards in the workplace; and a bill that established the Department of Consumer Affairs to protect the interests of consumers.

Nineteen sixty-eight not only marked Gallagher's re-election, but also the beginning of the Nixon presidency, Nixon having been elected on a law-and-order platform and a six-point plan to end the war in Vietnam. There was a relationship between Nixon and Hoover that went as far back as the Hiss case in 1948, when Nixon became the youngest member of the HUAC. Unable to convict State Department official Alger Hiss of espionage, the committee went after him for perjury. Secretly supported by Hoover, Nixon spearheaded the investigation, finally proving the charge that Hiss was a Soviet spy by linking stolen documents to Hiss' Woodstock typewriter, then dramatically presenting the evidence to a grand jury.

Hiss was convicted of perjury and sentenced to four years in prison, catapulting the young congressman into national prominence. Though Nixon denied FBI complicity, an FBI operative later revealed that Nixon had been given evidence by his friends at the FBI. More astonishing, Hiss asserted that the Woodstock typewriter that convicted him wasn't his and that a forgery had been committed despite the fact that Nixon claimed that a typewriter is like a fingerprint and that even his most ardent critics would not believe such a charge.[2]

But typewriters had been forged and, as early as 1941, the

Office of Strategic Services (OSS) had developed machines that could faultlessly reproduce the imprint of any typewriter in the world, using that capability in anti-Nazi sting operations during World War II. More damning were Nixon's words that drew a parallel between his ITT dilemma at the time and the Hiss case. "The typewriters are always the key. We had one built in the Hiss case,"[3] he said.

From his position, Hoover watched every minute of Nixon's career from then on: his Senate campaign against Helen Gahagan Douglas, the Khrushchev Kitchen Debate, his narrow loss to John Kennedy for the presidency, his failed comeback against Governor Pat Brown in California. This was Hoover's man: paranoid, flawed, thirsty for power and virulently anti-Communist. More, from behind the scenes, Hoover had fed him secret and confidential information on political opponents and enemies whenever it was needed. In short, Gallagher asserts, Hoover had made him.

In 1968, Nixon succeeded, suppressing his own self-destructive tendencies long enough to win the presidency. To Gallagher, the pairing of Hoover and Nixon was frightening. By October 1970, they'd put together a schedule of anti-crime measures titled the Organized Crime Bill, which called for mandatory federal registration of all persons and institutions dispensing drugs; the coordination of state and local law enforcement departments with twenty-five federal agencies to target individuals for investigation; the creation of a centralized national data bank to compile files on known and suspected criminals and their associates; and the controversial "No Knock" policy, which allowed police to enter private homes without warning when they suspected criminal activities were in progress.

Gallagher objected and, along with twenty-five other Democratic congressmen, voted against the bill. But in the government of the day, Gallagher claims, once a legislator labeled a policy anti-crime, almost everyone in Congress saw political advantage in jumping on the bandwagon regardless of it implications.

A key reason law enforcement officials advocated the passage of the "No Knock" policy was that drug dealers would flush illegal narcotics down toilets when the police arrived. After listening to their testimony, it seemed to Gallagher that the problem wasn't in the need to gain entry, but in the toilets. So, protesting a philosophy that refused to deal with the problem of street crime, the prevention and cure of drug addiction and anti-poverty legislation to attack crime at its source, Gallagher proposed the "No Flush" policy, which would provide a $500 fine for anyone having indoor plumbing.

By 1970 proposals by men like Tom Charles Huston, former national chairman of Young Americans for Freedom, began suggesting programs that Gallagher saw as blatantly unconstitutional. Titled the Huston Plan, the program united the intelligence agencies in order to share information. On June 5, 1970, Huston met with Hoover, among others, at Nixon's request. The premise was "everything is valid, everything is possible."[4] The interagency strategies that developed involved using listening devices, intercepting domestic mail when necessary and the use of on-campus informants to monitor university dissidents and revolutionary leaders. Among the first targets was the Brookings Institute, a liberal think tank, which was thought to have valuable studies on the Vietnam War, campus dissidents and radical African Americans.

On July 14, 1969, Nixon approved the program, establishing Huston as its focal point, but reconsidered when Hoover went to Attorney General John Mitchell to complain. The reversal threw Huston into a rage. He claimed in an August 5 memo that Hoover was fearful of anything that might jeopardize his autonomy. But Huston's legacy lived on in a way he could not have anticipated, Gallagher argues. Intelligence people who knew the president and his four intelligence chiefs had backed away from a showdown with Hoover.

The idea for the White House to take over and run police functions itself proved irresistible to members of the Committee to Re-Elect the President (CREEP), Gallagher believes. CREEP's mission, in addition to Nixon's re-election, was to overturn, either by judicial decree or constitutional amendment, the law prohibiting presidents to hold office for more than two terms, thus allowing Nixon to run for a third term using any means necessary.

# THE PRIVACY WAR

# XXIX
# Behavioral Modification

**"...300,000 boys and girls, ages 6 to 16, were at the time taking some form of psychotic drug."**

Continuing his investigation, in 1970, Gallagher learned of a program that tested the blood of grammar school boys in Baltimore to identify the chromosome XYY, which was associated with delinquency. In April of that year, a psychiatrist close to Nixon used his contacts with the president to propose the testing of children between the ages of six and eight to determine their propensity toward juvenile delinquency. It was proposed as an anti-crime measure, Gallagher learned, and received a $5 million grant from the Department of Health, Education and Welfare.

"All children should be tested. The younger, the better," explained the doctor. "Those found to be disturbed would be relocated, then put in group therapy units because individual therapy is expensive and they conform better in a group. Government run children's camps, monitored by behavioral psychologists, are to the benefit of the child, his parents and the nation. The voluntary approach is the most desirable. If there is resistance, then we have a problem that needs legislation."[1]

At the privacy hearing held on this topic, Gallagher asked the doctor how accurate his test was. The doctor replied that it was 90 percent accurate. Gallagher did some fast figuring. According to his calculations there would be 200,000 American children between the ages of six and eight, in these "concentration camps," a term the doctor protested, explaining that they were not concentration camps but rehabilitation camps.

On April 14, 1970, the congressman entered seven seminal statements into the Congressional Record regarding the plan, along with the federally funded STARR program, which Gallagher believed targeted young African Americans in an attempt to answer to racial problems in America.

> Mr. Speaker, I have inserted several statements that describe plans and actions which have taken place since my privacy subcommittee began its investigation. I would call special attention to the article by Miss Judith Randall, a prize-winning reporter for the *Washington Star*. She makes the point that conformity is as deadly as any of the pollutions now undergoing scrutiny at all levels of government. I am delighted that she says substantially the same thing I have said during the six years I've been concerned with invasion of privacy.

> And privacy is now under massive attack. This is why I also insert a statement on the subject of testing 6,000 young men confined to Maryland's correction institutions and 7,200 boys, age 2 to 18, from underprivileged Negro families in East Baltimore, for an XYY chromosome. I would merely comment that while HEW was rejecting a proposal that could result in preordained doom because of what a child saw in an ink blot, it is funding dozens of studies that may do the same thing over a drop of blood.

> Further, I call your attention to the statements...published in the *Journal of the American Medical Association* calling for a program of massive screening of American citizens, "That poverty and inade-

quate education underlie the nation's urban riots is well known, but the obviousness of these causes has blinded us to the role of brain dysfunction in the rioters who engage in arson, sniping and physical assault. There is evidence that brain dysfunction plays a significant role in the violent and assaultive behavior of as many as 10 million individuals in the United States. Individuals with electroencephalographic abnormalities in the temporal region have been found to have a much greater frequency of behavioral abnormalities. Our greatest danger no longer comes from famine or communicable diseases, but from ourselves and what lies within our fellow humans. For this reason we need to develop an 'early warning test' of limbic brain function to detect those humans who have a low threshold for impulsive violence. Violence is a public health problem, and the major thrust of any program dealing with violence must be toward its prevention."

Mr. Speaker, I am confident that tomorrow's newspapers will bring to light proposals of equal horror containing similar dangers for a free society. I have proposed the creation of a Select Committee on Technology, Human Values, and Democratic Institutions for precisely this reason. I believe Congress must have a fully funded committee whose sole purpose is to look beneath the surface of plans such as I have described in opposition to what appears to me to be the present campaign against the human spirit here in America. I would urge my colleagues to look with favor upon the creation of such a committee.[2]

Among these revelations, Gallagher uncovered evidence that Harvard psychologist B. F. Skinner's experiments in behavioral modification and his book, *Beyond Freedom and Dignity*, which followed, had been funded a total of $283,000 over nearly a decade by the National Institute of Mental Health.[3] Skinner said in his defense, "My image in some places is of a monster of some kind who wants to pull a string and manipulate people. Nothing could be further from the truth. People are manipulated; I just want them to be manipulated more effectively."[4]

These were, without a doubt, strange times. A short few months before, the United States put Neil Armstrong on the moon. The war in Vietnam was escalating. The aftermath of the Kent State University killing of four unarmed students by National Guard troops was smoldering. Information forwarded at Gallagher's request from the General Accounting Office disclosed that there were 70,000 grants within the Department of Health, Education and Welfare, 10,000 with the Department of Labor and an undisclosed number of behavioral research grants funded by the Department of Defense. When he requested a review of funds given by the government for psychological research, he was told that the task was virtually impossible. In other words, Gallagher concluded, Congress, for the most part, was unaware of how it's research money was being spent.

In hearings beginning in early 1970 and concluding on September 29 of the same year, Gallagher's subcommittee studied federal involvement in the use of behavior modification drugs on grammar school children. They discovered that in the early 1970s, 300,000 boys and girls, ages six to sixteen, were at the time taking some form of psychotic drug including Ritalin, Dexedrine, Deaner, Aventyl and Tofranil, many as part of federally funded programs. Twelve different drugs in all were identified. In some cases, individual students had been put on as many as ten different drugs during the course of a single school year without parental consent.[5]

In startling conclusion the subcommittee wrote, "The inference that can be drawn from these hearings is that minority groups are, in fact, the targets of the STAAR program. Literally hundreds of studies resulting from continuous research and investigation support the notion that poor educational achievement among the socially and economically deprived, more often than not, is attributable to inferior or outdated textbooks, watered down curricula, inadequate facilities, incompetent teachers, and the ills associated with the 'poverty cycle.' Second, the introduction of behavioral modification drugs is perceived to be another step in the process of controlling specific groups of people."[6]

But the true impact of the committee's conclusion didn't strike Gallagher until months later when he came into possession of a top-secret document regarding the survival of American society and the most "dispensable" segments of the United States population in the event of nuclear war or other catastrophes. Caucasian men and women were ranked least "dispensable" with regard to keeping the society viable after a catastrophic event. African Americans and homosexuals ranked most "dispensable," with a host of others in between.

# THE PRIVACY WAR

## XXX
## The Indictment of Mayor John Kenny

**"They can call me into courts any damn time they want."**

The study gave Gallagher pause in much the same way as the Warren Report had done eight years earlier for Jim Garrison. Yet, just as the subcommittee's work on children and behavioral-modification drugs was making headlines, an unbounded victory occurred for him. He was attending a campaign rally for Jersey City mayor Tom Whelan when he heard the news from a group of reporters. A statement had been issued that afternoon saying that the House Ethics Committee found no evidence of any wrongdoing on Gallagher's part in the *Life* magazine allegations. The inquiry into the congressman's affairs was officially closed.

It was strange for Gallagher, needless to say, surrounded by reporters and learning of the news and that his anguishes over the previous eight months were so suddenly ended. "To say I'm delighted is probably the greatest understatement I can make," Gallagher told the press. "I said all along I welcomed the investigation. The happy part is that I was re-elected. How sad it would be to have dropped out, which was the intent of the whole smear, and then to be cleared."

Two months later, the Hudson County prosecutor, James Tumulty, who'd charged a grand jury to investigate the magazine's allegations against Gallagher, sent jurors home citing a dearth of credible evidence.

Shortly after in January 1969, Gallagher was presented the Franklin Peace Medal for his efforts on behalf of nuclear disarmament and the creation of world peace. "The work of attaining a just and lasting peace is never complete," he told a Washington audience, which included Rick and his four daughters. "Man can do much, he can reach out to the stars, he can explore the ocean depths. He has found ways to conquer disease, and to triumph over ignorance, but despite these vast accomplishments, he has still not found a way to live with his fellow man. Finding a way to do that is the great unfinished business of the human race."

During the next four months, Gallagher was appointed congressional advisor to the Arms Control and Disarmament Agency, selected chairman of the House Foreign Affairs Committee on Asian Pacific Affairs and renamed chairman of the U.S.-Canada Interparliamentary Conference. Finally, it seemed, he'd broken loose from the controversy surrounding him to pursue his first love, foreign affairs. But soon enough, controversy again found him. Information that Gallagher's subcommittee gathered, such as the use of behavioral-modification drugs on children, could not be ignored.

The media ran with the stories, which led the way to FBI investigations into Gallagher. He simply could not break free from the allegations. Subpoenas were issued for the court appearances of Zicarelli, Angelo DeCarlo, Sam DeCavalante and dozens of others, including some who had nothing to do with the scandal.[1] In October 1970, after two years of investigation, seventy-seven-year-old John Kenny was also indicted by a U.S. grand jury.

Later that month, the Hudson County Democratic Party held a $100 a plate dinner for Kenny at the Jersey City armory attended by 3,500 people. Always a big boxing fan, Kenny, flanked by boxing greats Mickey Walker, Willie Pep, Ernie Durando and Joey Giardello, exhorted a cheering crowd of loyal friends and supporters.

"I'm not afraid when they say, 'You're indicted!' After all, what is an indictment? It just means that somebody's lied about you and as far as I'm concerned they can call me into courts any damn time they want."[2]

The next day, U.S. marshals raided the county treasurer's office and confiscated more than $300,000 in proceeds from the fund-raiser as "evidence."[3]

Upon returning from the dinner, Rick put their girls to bed and she and Gallagher sat at the kitchen table talking about Kenny's indictment and the pressure being exerted on them. Rick voiced her concern about everyone believing they were criminals regardless of Gallagher's charges being cleared. Gerry Ford spoke to Richard Kleindienst, Nixon's attorney general, about his situation, he explained to her. Ford asked to have the controversy stopped. He wanted Kleindienst's agents at the Justice Department, the IRS and FBI to decide once and for all if he was guilty of any crime.

"Kleindienst said 'Listen,'" Gallagher explained. "'You stay away from that guy if you know what's good for you. He's bad news with a lot of powerful enemies who'll come after you next if you don't wise up and stay out of this.'"

How badly did they want him? In 1990 through the Freedom of Information Act, Gallagher was able to procure Department of Treasury document "5-48-8226 RE: Cornelius E. Gallagher," written February 25, 1972, by the IRS. It was an official letter that read "Please be advised that 11 agents in addition to the four agents that conducted the original investigation were assigned to assist U.S. Attorney Herbert Stern and Attorney Harlow Huckabee as of

Thursday, February 24, 1972. Any additional assistance required by the Service will be readily available."[4]

While the dangers of pursuing his Privacy Hearings could not have been more clear than at this time, the issue itself was turning mainstream, demonstrated by the July 27, 1970, *Newsweek* cover story, "Is Privacy Dead?" The six-page article highlighted much of the subcommittee's work in regulating retail credit information, and curtailing wiretaps, bugs and the National Data Bank Concept. The magazine stated that Gallagher "fought the lone fight for privacy for five years on a single Congressional appropriation of $65,000, the most economical campaign since Joshua's at Jericho."[5]

Flattering, but necessarily superficial. Reporters could use only pieces of the hearings because they were held in closed sessions. Yet, probably their most significant finding was a Pentagon plan to ship 27,000 tons of lethal VX gas from arsenals in Colorado and Maryland to Elizabeth, N.J. From there, the gas was to be loaded onto obsolete World War II Liberty ships and sunk 250 miles out to sea. This was Gallagher's first contact with the darkest, most chilling, element of the Cold War and America's future: chemical and biological warfare.

# XXXI
# Bioweapons

**"The goal was to create a disease for which there was no cure."**

The investigation began during hearings that Gallagher was chairing for the House Foreign Affairs Committee concerning a State Department report on the international development of ocean resources in May 1969. The driving force behind these hearings was ecological responsibility, so when Gallagher learned of army operations where deadly gasses such as phosgene, VX and mustard gas were being disposed of in the Atlantic Ocean, he was beside himself.

Within one week, Gallagher summoned representatives from the U.S. Army to testify. From the testimony he was shocked to learn that during the late 1960s dozens of similar train-to-sea operations had taken place. During these transports, thousands of tons of lethal gases were shipped via railcar from military arsenals in Colorado, Maryland, Arkansas and Kentucky to the East Coast where they were loaded onto cargo ships to be sunk in the Atlantic.

Coincidentally, at the time, Richard McCarthy, congressman from New York, had seen a television documentary on biological and gas warfare that prompted him to seek information on U.S. national policy regarding the testing and disposal of these weapons.

He and Gallagher met to compare notes and learned that without sanction or communication with the State Department, Department of Interior or local authorities, the U.S. Army had been disposing of obsolete weapons for years in this manner. More horrifying, they learned that a 27,000-ton shipment was scheduled for June of that year in Gallagher's district. The weapons included 1,700 "coffins" of mustard gas, 12,540 rockets loaded with phosgene and 21,000 clusters of "bomblets" filled with VX,162, a nerve gas so lethal that less than a milligram had the potential to kill an adult human.[1]

In a closed session before his subcommittee, Gallagher learned that the train-to-sea method was considered the safest way to dispose of the materials. But the more they investigated the subject, the more it appeared anything but safe. The plan was to avoid highly populated areas, yet the seventy-car train would pass through Indianapolis; Dayton; Philadelphia; and Elizabeth, New Jersey.

Gallagher asked about the possibility of derailment, the rupture of a tank or a terrorist attack. He noted that only two years earlier, 20 cars of a 120 car caravan derailed spilling ammonia gas, which drifted into the town of Crete, Nebraska, and killed eight people. If that were VX gas the results would be tragic. With regard to the ocean environment, his original source of concern, it was asserted that the weapons would be sealed in canisters, then sunk 7,200 feet to the ocean floor. Even if a "coffin" did leak, the gas would be active for no more than 185 hours and would take 400 years to reach the surface. But, again, the logic was not compelling and the military's track record regarding issues of public safety not credible to Gallagher.

The congressman reminded them of the SS *John Harvey* catastrophe of 1942, a top-secret mission to deliver 2,000

M47A1 chemical bombs to Bari, Italy. Before the ship could
unload, a brutal twenty-minute Luftwaffe attack on the harbor
sank seventeen Allied vessels including the *John Harvey*, which
underwent two explosions, one from a German bomb, the second from its cargo of chemical weapons. Smoke polluted with
the chemical contaminated the town. The worst casualties
weren't the thousands who inhaled the fumes, but the sailors
whose bodies were immersed in the chemical. No one knew anything about the true cargo the *John Harvey* was carrying since the
captain was killed in the explosion.

The morning following the disaster, many claimed to be
blind. Reddish-brown burns developed over their bodies, which
stripped their top layers of skin. Some men were reported to have
90 percent skin loss. Victims' lungs and respiratory tracts were left
without lining. In the town itself there were similar scenes of misery. More than 1,000 civilians were killed, some from the poison-
ous cloud that hovered over the town, others after coming into
contact with the chemical on shore.[2]

The recounting of the *John Harvey* episode left a pall in the
air, but there were other episodes, more current and alarming, that
Gallagher would eventually learn of. Still, given even the limited
amount of information, Congressman McCarthy and he, convinced that public health was in danger, went public with the plan,
creating a massive outcry.

Finally, with public pressure mounting, the Pentagon agreed
to allow a civilian panel of experts from the National Academy of
Sciences to study the situation to determine whether there existed
an alternate method of deactivating the weapons that was less haz-
ardous to the public. Six weeks later, the panel came out against
the army's train-to-sea method recommending that a detoxifica-
tion process be undertaken on site at the weapon arsenals. Though

the Pentagon capitulated, the American public was more frightened than ever because they now knew that these weapons existed. They were being tested, stored and disposed of often only a few miles from their homes.

Gallagher also learned in March 1968 that a Pentagon-sponsored VX plant was manufacturing thousands of tons of the gas annually and loading it into land mines, artillery shells and aircraft spray tanks. Even more ominous, developments in biological warfare were beginning, which would have enormous effects on the future.

From his inquiries, Gallagher learned that as early as the 1940s, certain plants were producing biological weapons at a rate of 250,000 Type F, four-pound bombs per month, which were filled with self-cultivated botulinus toxin. The stockpile of biological weapons developed over that period was awesome, and to this day there are areas around these plants so contaminated with pathogens related to Lassa fever virus, Ebola virus, tularemia and Q fever that they're permanently off-limits to human beings.[3]

Though this was horrific to Gallagher, it was in the field of biological warfare that the most frightening possibilities had presented themselves over the years. Since the discovery of the double helix in 1953, scientists' understanding of genetics facilitated the development of an ethnic weapon, a biological weapon designed to target selected racial groups. An example of this occurred during the Vietnam War when an elite group of scientists working for the Pentagon had carried out blood tests on selected groups of Asians to prepare "a map portraying the geographic distribution of human blood groups and other inherited blood characteristics."[4] With this information scientists could lock on to genetic signatures and create a weapon that segregated those genetically vulnerable to it from those who were not. Equally possible was the ability, based on gene splicing or recombinant DNA, to manufacture new diseases that could accomplish the same end. One CIA doctor described the work of a subordinate who bombarded bacteria with ultraviolet radiation in order to create deviant strains. "We were working with the manipulation of genes and genetic reengineering of viruses as early as 1965.... The goal was to create diseases for which there was no cure."[5]

In September 1969, a Department of Defense spokesman elaborated on the subject while testifying before the House Appropriations Committee. "Unlike most chemicals," he said, "biological agents cannot be separated from a natural habitat, and may not be recognized until after they have caused widespread infection. The likelihood of early warning and detection of their presence is virtually nil within the next five to ten years."[6]

*Newsweek*, in its May 7, 1984, issue, pictured a world map showing arrows pointing to probable routes of the AIDS virus on the move out of central Africa.[7] What the *Newsweek* roadmap forgot to mention, Gallagher points out, was the theory that the AIDS virus originated in the African green monkey, then "jumped" species through monkey or insect bites, the ingestion of contaminated meat or bestiality into the human population. From there, it later spread from Africa to Haiti and eventually to Manhattan.

The first serious attack against the green monkey theory came from the Soviets in a commentary aired from Moscow on December 25, 1985. The piece ended with the weighty, if not totally unexpected, conclusion that the AIDS epidemic was caused by experiments carried out in the United States as part of the development of new biological weapons.[8] Nine months later an article in the August 1986 issue of the *Journal of the Royal Society of Medicine* advised scientists to think most carefully about the Soviet statements. In 1978, scientists in virus laboratories had already performed experiments with sheep visna viruses. They were passed into human brain cells, which allowed them to "jump" into a new species, namely homo sapiens. The result was that anyone with access to the virus could initiate an epidemic.[9]

On May 11, 1987, the *London Times* published an explosive front-page story, "Smallpox Vaccine Triggered AIDS Virus," which proposed that a smallpox eradication program sponsored by the World Health Organization (WHO) was responsible for unleashing AIDS in Africa. Almost 100 million Black Africans living in central Africa were inoculated. The vaccine, the article contended, was responsible for awakening a dormant AIDS virus infection on the continent. In that article, Dr. Robert Gallo admitted that the connection between the WHO program and the epidemic was interesting. Though he could not say that it actually happened, he had been contending for years that the use of live vaccines could easily activate a dormant infection such as HIV.[10]

Male homosexuals living in large urban centers have borne the brunt of the epidemic. Beyond that, the other most susceptible groups are prostitutes, drug users, Haitians, and hemophiliacs. Instances of the disease among African Americans is disproportionately high. Fifty percent of children with AIDS are Black; 25 percent are Hispanic. To find situations analogous to the proposition that the AIDS virus was manufactured and then dispensed to target groups through inoculations, Gallagher reminds us of the Tuskegee Syphilis Experiment.

Who or what was responsible for starting AIDS: the African green monkey or germ-warfare scientists? Was it the military, biological warfare experts or the CIA? Over the years in his dealings with each of the agencies that might be responsible, Gallagher believes in the possibility that AIDS was created and spread, either purposefully or accidentally, through the government-sponsored genetic-engineering programs he fought to eradicate.

# THE PRIVACY WAR

# XXXII
## Boggs' Mission

**"The time has come for the attorney general of the United States to ask for the resignation of Mr. Hoover."**

In April 1971, Hale Boggs met with Gallagher in a private meeting. "A telephone company repairman came by my house the other day and pulled this out of my home phone," Boggs said holding up a small black item, a listening device. "Seems now that since Mitchell and Nixon have had the Anti-Eavesdropping Bill overruled, anybody's fair game."

Gallagher was in the House chamber the next morning and so was almost everyone else who had ever voiced concern about Hoover, the federal government and the privacy issue, all of them knowing that something significant was about to happen. But none, not even Carl Albert, was aware of exactly what Boggs was about to do. So, when he stood to address the chamber, the packed room was silent.

"Mr. Speaker and my colleagues, what I am going to say I say in sorrow because it is always tragic when a great man who has given his life to his country comes to the twilight of his life and fails to understand it is time to leave the service and enjoy retirement.

"Mr. Speaker, I am talking about J. Edgar Hoover, the director of the Federal Bureau of Investigation. The time has come for the attorney general of the United States to ask for his resignation."

Speculation spread through the chamber. No one could believe it. But Boggs continued.

"When the FBI taps the telephones of members of this body and members of the Senate, when the FBI stations agents on college campuses to infiltrate college organizations, when the FBI adopts the tactics of the Soviet Union and Hitler's Gestapo, then it is time—it is way past time—Mr. Speaker, that the present director no longer be the director. I ask again now that you have enough courage to demand the resignation of this man."

Carl Albert's face was ashen. John Rooney and Pete Rodino were too shocked to speak. A string of speakers came to the director's aid. But despite the support for Hoover, Gallagher saw this moment as the first thread coming loose in the suit, one that would be tugged by others like him until the myth surrounding the man finally came undone.

In the days that followed, Boggs pushed hard for the resignation. Within Congress he failed miserably. Outside the federal government, however, Boggs' speech, coupled with revelations about COINTELPRO and other secret government operations, scored points with journalists who began to smell something rotten in the federal law-enforcement institutions.

It began with an article by Ron Kessler in the *Washington Post* titled, "FBI Wiretapping: How Widespread?" The story then blossomed into a ten-page *New York Times Magazine* feature, "What Have They Done Since They Shot Dillinger?" by Tom Wicker, which was highly critical of Hoover and the agency. This was followed by a series of exposés by Jack Anderson that were syndicated in newspapers nationwide from April through September of 1971.

The Wicker story, replete with episode after episode demonstrating Hoover's iron-fisted governing of the bureau, overt racism and rampant abuses of power, struck a nerve with the public. Not only did it offer a fascinating insight into the man, documented with real incidents and people, but it stirred their imagination to wonder that if this was public knowledge, what was being kept secret.

If Wicker's allegations warmed the soup, Jack Anderson's September 22, 1971, column left it scalding, opening with, "J. Edgar Hoover, the old bulldog of the FBI, has just bared his fangs." From there, he launched into a list of charges that stated Hoover had collected more than $250,000 in royalties from three books that were researched and written for him by FBI personnel on government time, spent summer vacations in $110-a-day suites and assigned agents to monitor politicians including Gallagher.[1]

Soon after, exacerbated by the director's refusal to support the Huston Plan and use of the FBI to uncover the Watergate scandal, Nixon began to fall out of love with Hoover. In late December 1971, just months before Watergate, Nixon invited Hoover to the White House ostensibly to be told he could stay on only until after the election when a new FBI director would be appointed. But the discussion didn't go that way. Something happened. Many suppose it was blackmail built around the director's knowledge of secret operations carried out by Nixon's Plumbers. Whatever occurred during that meeting, the president later told John Ehrlichman, "We may have on our hands here a man who will pull down the temple with him, including me."[2]

And that was it. J. Edgar Hoover had, at least for the time being, again survived, despite the best efforts of Gallagher, Hale Boggs, Jack Anderson, Tom Wicker, John Ehrlichman and the president himself.

In addition to Boggs' mission to bring down Hoover, he

strove to re-open investigations on the assassinations of the Kennedys and King, believing they were all linked and part of a massive cover-up. The house majority Leader would again fail, though he did inspire others such as Rep. Allard Lowenstein from New York and Sen. Frank Church of Idaho. Boggs and others like Jim Garrison continued to hammer away at inconsistencies in the Warren Commission report and connections they attempted to document between Oswald; CIA operatives David Ferrie, Clay Shaw and Guy Bannister; and Sam Giancana and Johnny Roselli.

While Boggs, Garrison and many others questioned the Warren Commission's lone assassin theory, Lowenstein was implacable in his efforts to get behind the theory as it related to King and especially Bobby Kennedy, with whom he'd shared a close personal relationship. "I do not know why those responsible for law enforcement in Los Angeles decided to stonewall the RFK case," he said at a press conference at the Statler Hilton in Manhattan. "But once they had made that decision, facts had to be distorted and inconvenient evidence done away with; inoperative statements had to be replaced by new statements; people raising awkward questions had to be discredited, preferably as self-seeking or flaky."[3]

In the end, Church's Assassinations Committee would conclude that both James Earl Ray and Sirhan Sirhan were lone gunmen engaged in solitary acts, but finally conceding that the assassination of John Kennedy was most likely a conspiracy planned by the Mafia.[4]

And it was the Mafia, according to many, that was blackmailing Hoover. Mafiosi from Sam Giancana to Frank Costello, according to Bill Bonanno, son of former crime boss Joseph Bonanno, controlled the FBI director. Bill Bonanno recalled an incident that occurred at Roy Cohn's office in 1966:

One day, I and a couple of captains from our family paid a visit to Roy Cohn, the attorney who, over the years, had maintained bridges between our world and the government. "Ever see these?" Cohn said, untying the stay and removing a batch of photos. There were seven or eight of them. Most were five-by-seven shots, a couple were eight-by-ten photos. They were all pictures of Hoover in women's clothing. His face was daubed with lipstick and makeup and he wore a wig of ringlets. In several of the photos, he posed alone, smiling, even mugging for the camera. In a few other photos, he was sitting on the lap of an unidentified male, stroking his cheek in one, hugging him in another, holding a morsel of food before his mouth in yet another.[5]

While Boggs moved in one direction continuing his efforts to shake loose from Hoover and re-open investigation into the assassinations, Gallagher moved in another. Sick of the negativity, Justice Department hounding and lack of progress in putting forward the day-to-day work of Congress, he worked harder than he'd ever worked before.

# THE PRIVACY WAR

RON FELBER

## XXXIII
## Gallagher Overseas

**"He'd never seen anything as bad as the rebellion."**

Shortly after Boggs' speech, Gallagher remembers contemplating his own path while at the Chandelier restaurant in Bayonne with Rick, Neil Carroll and his oldest daughter, Diane, who was just out of college at the time. He complained about how frustrated he was to be tied up with the continuous investigations, that if it wasn't the allegations regarding Barney O'Brien, it was an international conspiracy of some kind involving Balaguer or Zicarelli. Frankly, he didn't want to talk about assassinations or Hoover any more.

Diane studied him for a moment. "You know, Dad," she said, "you should grow your hair a little longer. That's what I do when I feel like I'm in a rut. I change my hairstyle. I'm like a new person with a new attitude."

"I wish it were that easy," Gallagher responded, but Rick agreed with Diane.

"Maybe she's right, Neil. Maybe a new look would motivate you."

Gallagher didn't pay much attention to the idea initially, but soon found himself skipping haircuts. Beyond the new hairstyle, however, and despite the best efforts of the U.S.

**239**

Attorney's Office, the coming months proved to be Gallagher's most productive in Congress.

In the time that followed, Gallagher's bill calling for $101 million to construct drug-rehabilitation centers in urban areas passed the House 399-0. The Subcommittee on Privacy halted a second attempt by the U.S. Army and the FBI called CONUS to maintain computer files on U.S. citizens. A United Nations drive, initiated by him, through a correspondence with Soviet president Alexi Kosygin to combine medical talents and knowledge in an international battle against cancer did, in fact, begin an extended scientific discourse between the Soviet Union and the United States to work toward a cure for the disease. Additionally, a speech he'd written titled "Technology and Society: Conflict of Interest?" was selected by the Institute of Management Sciences as one of the five "Vital Speeches" of that year.

The work he was most proud of though didn't focus on legislating new forward-looking ideas, but on stopping genocide as perpetrated by Pakistan against the East Bengalis of what was then East Pakistan in mid-1971. As chairman of the House Asian and Pacific Affairs Committee, he began hearings on the subject, but felt it was his moral obligation to personally investigate the stories of terror and barbarity they'd been uncovering on an almost daily basis.

So, in June he traveled to India, visiting some of the six million evacuees living in makeshift camps set up beyond the Pakistani border, later addressing members of the Calcutta Press Club with his findings concerning the enormity of the situation. He faced a barrage of questions on the role of the U.S. government in East Pakistan and attempted to convince newsmen that the American president was concerned with the problems there, pointing out that the U.S. government was the first to respond to the appeal of the secretary general of the United Nations, U. Thant of Myanmar, by contributing substantially to the aid fund for the victims of the tragedy.

Gallagher's reaction to seeing the results of Pakistan's success in putting down the Bengali rebellion in East Pakistan was one of sheer horror. In World War II, he'd seen the worst battlefields of France—the killing grounds in Normandy—but he'd never seen anything as bad as in this rebellion: babies with their arms ripped off, young girls raped and mutilated, men and women butchered on the spot. He later learned that the State Department and CIA had been covertly supporting President Yahya Khan's subsidized slaughter. In any case, he left with two convictions based on humanitarian, if not military, objectives: The world community needed urgently to bring emergency relief to those refugee camps, and all foreign aid should immediately be cut off to Pakistan until President Khan brought some semblance of humanity into his country's government.

In the days that followed, over President Nixon's objections, Gallagher led efforts to direct $45 million in emergency aid to starving Bengali refugees, $17.5 million of which came from the United States. By mid-June, ten days after his tour of the camps, he'd written an amendment to the 1971-1972 Foreign Aid Bill demanding a halt to $445 million in economic and military aid slated for Pakistan and a total embargo on arms shipments to that country. The House Foreign Affairs Committee passed the amendment 17 votes to 6, with the full House voting 200 to 192 in its favor. These legislative actions saved millions of lives and paved the way for the creation of the sovereign state of Bangladesh five months later.

The next week in a speech before Congress, Gallagher called for the diplomatic reorganization of Bangladesh as a new nation.

He was the first official in the United states to move for supporting a new independent nation of eighty million people.

# XXXIV
# Tocks Island

**"This virtually ensured Gallagher's removal from Congress."**

The sizzling pace he'd established for himself in Congress proved therapeutic, but even that wasn't enough to make him forget the nonstop investigations, which had been going on now for more than four years. The *New York Post* again questioned whether Gallagher was politically tied to Zicarelli and supported Hoover's assertion that bugs were never planted. Subsequently, in April 1971, the *Post* proposed that if Gallagher had been elected as vice president, America would have a Mobster in the White House.[1]

On April 26, 1971, Gallagher's Subcommittee on Privacy was shut down. Perhaps he should have joined the chorus of others who accused him of abandoning his responsibility to protect American citizens, but believing that the Subcommittee's record spoke for itself, decided to direct his efforts toward drafting a bill that would create a permanent committee with a mission to "monitor the effects which technological advances have on our freedom as individuals."

However, in September 1971, a *New York Daily News* story retelling the *Life* magazine Zicarelli saga reached the judge who presided over a land deal debate Gallagher was involved in. The deal, from May of that year, involved land Gallagher owned in

Warren County, New Jersey, for fourteen years. The land was condemned by the federal government in order for the Tocks Island Dam to be built. According to the law, the land was assessed and all landowners paid according to that assessment. However, as a congressman, the federal court was required to decide the worth of Gallagher's property.

Implying that he was about to make a financial killing, Gallagher asserts that the judge arranged the hearing on the day Gallagher's Consumer Protection Bill came to the floor for a vote. When Gallagher asked for an alternate, the request was denied. Stating that Gallagher must have been a wealthy man to choose Congress over his court, the judge set the land's value at exactly one-third of what all other landowners received.

Despite being sidetracked by the Tocks Island deal, Gallagher brought his Privacy Bill to the House on February 8, 1972. Originally, the prospects for its passage looked excellent. It had a broad base of bilateral support from Boggs, the Majority Leader; Ed Koch of New York; Moe Udall of Utah; and even Gerry Ford. But this was before it was argued that the creation of a Privacy Committee overlapped with the responsibilities of their Judiciary Committee, whose job it was to oversee the FBI. However, monitoring the FBI was never the intent of Gallagher's resolution, and he vehemently argued against both the premise and outcome they were trying to guarantee:

> Mr. Speaker, several days ago this resolution appeared to have broad support. Now the issue of jurisdiction has been raised by the chairman of the Committee on the Judiciary. This resolution is about privacy, the many aspects of privacy, something that affects everything that this Congress does and something that affects the life of every single person in the United States.

Now that's a pretty broad order, but I want to remind every-one that unless we wake up and begin to deal with privacy, it may well be that the Congress itself will become irrelevant in the twi-light of this decade and the most important thing that Congressmen will do will be to have their picture taken out on the steps with graduation classes, for we are allowing ourselves to sleep through a time of America's greatest challenge to its freedom.

There would today be a national data bank, with the records of every American's contact with the Federal Government in a cen-tralized, computerized system, if the Privacy Subcommittee had not taken action in 1966.

In March of 1970 I learned that there was under consider-ation, at the highest levels of our Government, a proposal to give every American child a psychological test to determine his poten-tial criminality. The plan proposed to take those children who flunked and send them to rehabilitation camps. I branded those camps "American Dachaus" and immediately launched a full-scale investigation with my privacy inquiry.... The most important part of the technology of behavior is a choice by a superior person as to what is good behavior.... We see that those of us who believe in freedom and dignity are to have no chance to participate in the choice, the choice will be made by an elite who have contempt for individualism.

Once the decision as to what constitutes good behavior is made, there are powerful tools to be used by the elite to impose their view on the rest of us.

First would be the computer. If you can know everything about a man, you can devise exactly the right approach to convince him that loyalty demands exactly what the State wants and what the computer discloses can be manipulated personally in that man.

Second are drugs. My Privacy Subcommittee disclosed that

250,000 grammar school children are being fed Ritalin and other psychotic drugs to change their behavior. This in spite of the fact that everyone knows bright children are bored in most classrooms. Other drugs have been developed and are being used to change the moods and alter the ideas of people at every age.

Third is psycho surgery. These brain mutilation operations are now being used on troublesome grammar school children and on others, mostly women and elderly people, who deviate from what is allegedly "normal" behavior.

Shocking, yes, but it is happening and no one is doing anything about it.

The vote was a losing battle at this point despite that just four days before, according to Gallagher, the bill had enough support to pass. By the time the vote was over the bill went down in flames, 216 to 168 with 33 of the 35 Judiciary Committee members voting against the Privacy Committee. Later, one chairman admitted that Hoover threatened to indict his brother if he did not withdraw his support for the bill.

By April 1972 Gallagher was beginning to see his experiences with *Life* from 1967 to 1969 as the good old days compared with those of 1970 to 1972. The plan was brought about by the Republican legislature and implemented by a panel of three federal judges, including Gallagher's judge in the Tocks Island deal, to re-align New Jersey's fifteen congressional districts, which would threaten Gallagher's re-election chances and those of New Jersey's eight other Democratic congressmen. The state's congressional districts were to be reshaped to accomplish two basic purposes: protecting New Jersey's six Republican incumbents in the House and giving Republican candidates a good chance of winning at least two seats from the Democrats.

Then, informed that Gallagher was about to be indicted, the judge dissolved what was his 13th District, dividing it up between five others, while creating a new district, which they called the 13th, in another part of the state. The court had harangued Gallagher out of Congress. However, in the small part of his district that remained, Gallagher carried 78 percent of the vote.

Despite all this bad news, Gallagher would seek re-election in 1972 against incumbent Dominick Daniels in the 14th District. But these were political issues that he saw as secondary to the basic values he'd grown up with: loyalty, friendship, God and country, the virtues one needed to live by. So, when Gallagher heard that the "Little Guy," John Kenny, was hospitalized, ailing with chronic diabetes, he wasted no time and rushed to see him.

It was a crisp fall afternoon with winter's chill creeping into the air when Gallagher arrived at Jersey City Hospital, the complex Frank Hague built and Kenny later modernized. To many it was an institution, not only for those who lived in Hudson County, but on a state level, where it enjoyed a reputation for being one of the most up-to-date hospitals around.

He entered Kenny's cluttered room and saw him, drawn and pale, lying up in bed watching a game show on a 12" black-and-white television set. For years, there had been headline after headline about all of the power he wielded, all of the money he'd supposedly taken, all of the real estate he secretly owned. The spark returned to his eyes as soon as Gallagher walked in.

"I should check you first," Kenny joked. "Last week they got one of them to come up here wearing a wire to get something on me. They've been trying for three years with no conviction yet. They'll eventually get me for something, I suppose, unless I kick off first."

"Guys like you live to be a hundred," Gallagher chuckled and sat beside him. "I owe you a lot, John. I mean that. You helped me all through my career. You were my mentor."

Kenny chortled and looked away, but turned toward him again. "How could things have ever gone so wrong, Neil? Was it something I did or didn't do? Was I a bad man?"

To Gallagher, Kenny, right there and then, was the loneliest man in the world. This was the last time Gallagher would see him alive, the memory of which haunts him to this day. But it was the quiet rage he felt at the dogged harassment Kenny endured even to his final days that gave him the strength to fight back when on April 10, 1972, a federal Grand Jury indicted Gallagher on charges of conspiracy, perjury and federal income tax evasion.

RON FELBER

## XXXV
## The Mysterious Death of Hale Boggs

**"This is corruption at the highest levels."**

On the afternoon of April 11, 1972, reporters from the *Jersey Journal*, the *Bayonne Times*, ABC television, *Newsweek* and the *New York Times*, crowded outside Gallagher's Washington office for a news conference he'd called to answer questions about the indictment. They asked about Barney O'Brien and Zicarelli mostly. As usual, Gallagher took the fight to his accusers. Flanked by Chip Witter, his Washington assistant, and Neil Carroll, his resident secretary, he read from a written statement:

> To date, over $11 million in tax payer dollars have been spent to destroy me. I have undergone the most relentless investigation in modern political history for more than four years, ever since leaked Federal raw investigative files were handed to *Life*. Any citizen—office holder, local policeman, anyone—who disagrees with our new Caesars will be the victim of this terrible repression. I have spoken out against it for nine years and for four years my family and friends have been subjected to a terror equal only to the oppression in Nazi Germany. In the days to come, I shall speak out on this—I will name names.
>
> I expect to be re-elected, but perhaps more important, I will

**249**

lay out for the first time on the public record the full story of the new surveillance subculture and those who would pervert democracy in the lust for uncontrolled power.

The reporters continued to question him about other issues, including the possibility of his resignation. But for Gallagher this was neither the time nor the place. His moment would come just days later in a speech he gave on April 19 before the full House.

"We'll be the targets of unremitting attacks," he warned Rick as seriously as he ever had. "Everything will be out in the open. I'll be a man with no safe harbor, no country."

Rick placed her hand over his. "What can they do to us that they haven't done already?" she said. "And if it can get worse, don't you think they're on their way to doing it? I do because, like it or not, Neil, you've grabbed hold of something that goes straight to the soul of this country that people are just now starting to understand."

On the morning of April 19, Gallagher stood in the well of the House of Representatives before a packed chamber ready to release a most shocking skein of revelations. He would decry the erosion of individual freedom in the United States and declare his status as an enemy of the state publicly for the first time while describing to his fellow legislators how he'd arrived at this desperate point in his life and political career.

"Mr. Speaker, let me now tell my story," Gallagher began, and explained his knowledge, as chairman of the Privacy Subcommittee, concerning the political destruction Hoover unleashed. In cold, hard detail, Gallagher described the threats Cohn had made against him at the behest of Hoover, the FBI's harassment of Martin Luther King, the bugging of House Speaker John McCormack's congressional office, the *Life* magazine articles and the incredible revelations that had been presented to his sub-committee regarding U.S. Army, FBI, and CIA abuses of the constitutional rights of American citizens.

> This is corruption at the highest levels of the Federal Bureau of Investigation, and when I would not cooperate, and would not put a stop on my subcommittee's legitimate inquiries, in retaliation, every possible filth was used to force me from the Congress.
>
> So, Mr. Speaker, my colleagues, and my friends, this is the real-life story. I have lived with this for over four years, always expecting that the investigations would end and that I would be allowed to go on with my life and career. But, of course, they could never let it end and so persecution finally escalated to prosecution.
>
> And, in a strange way, I welcome the indictment. Now, I can speak freely, and I shall continue to speak out before any forum I can find. I will make additional speeches on the floor and I will say, today, off the floor what I have said on the floor. I will be happy to appear before any body and swear to the facts as I have described them.

Gallagher was at the top of his game. But this was all interrupted when on October 18, 1972, reports came to him that Boggs' twin-engine Cessna carrying himself and three others had disappeared over Peril Straight, Alaska, 75 miles southwest of Juneau en route to a campaign for Rep. Nick Begich. Nothing was mentioned in Congress regarding the possibility of foul play.

The majority leader of the United States House of Representatives had simply vanished one evening and no one concluded that his vendetta with Hoover and his previous five years in Congress fighting to re-open investigations into the Kennedy and King assassinations, might be a clue.

Boggs wasn't alone, Gallagher believes today. There were others who were involved in the politics of the day and who died just as mysteriously as Boggs. Guy Bannister, who was brought to trial by Jim Garrison as a conspirator in the JFK assassination, died of an apparent heart attack in 1964 with a .357 Magnum revolver beside him. David Ferrie, a CIA operative, died in 1967 from a possible suicide shortly before Garrison called him before a grand jury to testify on the JFK assassination. Chicago Mob boss Sam Giancana, believed to be involved in the JFK assassination, was shot through the head execution style while under FBI protective custody days before he was to testify before the Church Committee on Assassinations in 1977. Johnny Roselli, Chicago labor racketeer and possible conspirator in the JFK assassination, was shot through the head execution style with his body dismembered and placed in fifty-five gallon drums that were left floating off the Florida coast shortly after he testified before the Assassinations Committee in 1978. William Sullivan, Hoover's number-two man who headed up the JFK assassination investigation for the FBI was purportedly mistaken for a deer and shot and killed by the son of a New Hampshire state policeman in 1979. Rep. Allard Lowenstein, the seventh on Nixon's enemies list, who carried Boggs' flag forward to re-open the investigation into the Kennedy assassinations, was shot five times and killed in a New York law office by a deranged former colleague in 1980.

It would not be until early 1974, while imprisoned in Allenwood, along with Watergate conspirators, that Gallagher would come upon the shocking truth concerning Hoover's own death on May 2, 1972, just two weeks after the congressman went before the House demanding his impeachment.

Three days after Hoover's death, the men who were to break into Democratic Headquarters in Washington, D.C., moved into

Room 419 of the Howard Johnson Motel directly opposite the Watergate building which they would make famous. Three weeks later, they would attempt their first break-in and fail. Soon after that they would succeed, but they came away without having accomplished their primary mission of planting operational listening devices in strategic areas of the building. The third attempt was made on the night of June 17, and the men were arrested, paving the way for the resignation of President Nixon.

This was also the time in New Jersey's 14th District where, having been indicted on two counts of tax evasion, four of perjury and one of conspiracy, Gallagher was supposed to be fighting for his political life in the primary against Dominick Daniels. Instead, he was struggling to prove his innocence and stay out of federal prison and was unsuccessful on both counts. Weighed down by the indictment, badly outgunned and with his constituency spread among four separate districts, he lost to Daniels.

With regard to his war with the federal government, it was painful, drawn-out and ugly. He was now also faced with a four-year, $11 million investigation of the bank where he was director. Staffed with fifteen full-time federal agents who set up desks in the basement of the bank, they searched every piece of paper that had been processed since Gallagher had become a director.

It didn't end there. The owners of the bank quickly wound up on the wrong side of the investigation targeted at Gallagher and were threatened to be indicted on eighteen counts of fraud and conspiracy. As it stood, Gallagher's role since 1958, when he'd first become a director, was not to make deals but to use his standing in the community to encourage business, a rainmaker of sorts. Given that, and the fact that he tried to be meticulous about any potential conflicts of interest, there was little the teams of IRS agents could find in the way of wrongdoing.

The owners of the bank were told that they had nothing against them. "It's Gallagher we're after and if you don't want to have your bank taken away and be indicted yourselves, you'll help us find a way to get him."

The owners called in Gallagher's mortgage and a $12,000 outstanding loan that he'd co-signed for a constituent who'd defaulted. The bank was then forced to sue Gallagher in order to get depositions that would hurt his defense while pressing the court to move for a trial. According to Gallagher, each time he attempted to pay, the amount due was raised through fines until it exceeded $80,000, which he did not have, allowing the bank to foreclose on his Bayonne home.

The charges brought forward in the seven-count indictment against Gallagher were borne of the same manipulation, he believes. The $78,000 he was judged to owe as federal income tax was never his to use and was turned over to him by the Hudson County Democratic Party to invest in tax-free municipal bonds at the bank where he was director. The bonds were not purchased by him, but by the owners, with Gallagher signed on as a co-trustee along with a representative of the Hudson County Democratic organization.

When Gallagher's co-trustee died in 1968, it created a problem in that there were two warring factions in the party at the time. Rather than get in the middle of the controversy, or interplead them to the court, Gallagher had the bank hold onto the bonds. The bonds were still invested and uncashed with Gallagher acting as legal trustee. All of this was done with the blessing of both the late Hudson County chairman and Gallagher's co-trustee.

Gallagher later returned the entire sum to the court to determine the right party of interest without taking one penny of it. However, in December 1972, exhausted and seeing only one way of escaping the Justice Department's alleged war against him, Gallagher pleaded guilty to income tax evasion.

A six-month delay in sentencing was granted to ensure that someone other than his judge in the Tocks Island deal presided over this final judgment. Gallagher wrote James Coolahan, chief judge of the United States District Court, a letter detailing the history of his situation and urging in the strongest possible terms that his trial be overseen by another judge:

> I have devoted my life in two wars and fourteen years in Congress to the concept of an America with a sense of fairness even to the lowest criminal. My entire career has been spent, in the words of the *New York Times*, as "a fighter for civil liberties."
>
> I plead, beg and implore you to assign my case to an impartial judge, not only in my interest, but in the interest of your conscience, the conscience of a good man, and in the interest of the integrity of the Court.
>
> Respectfully,
>
> Cornelius E. Gallagher

At 7:00 P.M. on June 10, while clearing up some last-minute matters in his Washington office, Gallagher received a call from Rick. She was apparently upset. The *New York Daily News* headlined the story "Gallagher Sings for Feds." People were pouring into the house in disbelief. Gallagher had not seen the headline. "Don't believe any of it," he told Rick.

At 2:30 P.M. the following day, just four days before his sentencing, Gallagher called a news conference at his Capitol Hill office. In these days of Watergate media frenzy, Gallagher's privacy war were a showstopper. With *The Godfather* in the theaters, Nixon in China and *Apollo 17* on the moon, Gallagher's case had it all: Mafia, money and international intrigue. Every major newspaper and television network was ready and waiting for the latest development.

The congressman was no longer bound by a national gag order and could at last defend himself against the *Life* allegations. A swirl of anticipation swept through his congressional office, crowded with television cameras and sound equipment, as he began his public statement over the buzz of the reporters and speculation that filled the room.

> In this article, the U.S. Attorney asserts that I in some way cooperated with his office by giving testimony about others in return for consideration of leniency during my sentencing for income tax evasion later this week. This is absolutely false. There has been no such testimony or information given. I will be sentenced on the merits of my situation with no deal or quid pro quo asked for or received.
>
> Clearly, I have had great pressure on me to begin talking, and lying, if I wanted to keep from going to jail. And as the Watergate investigation moves to Congress, pressure from the Justice Department has intensified to discredit the leaders of Congress including Speaker Carl Albert, Majority Leader Tip O'Neil and Pete Rodino, chairman of the Judiciary Committee, which will soon conduct the impeachment hearing of President Nixon.
>
> There is no doubt in my mind that if I wanted to join in the efforts by volunteering damaging information about others in Congress or in New Jersey, I could have waltzed out of my own legal problems long ago. But I believe, regardless of my own position, it is essential for the country that the Congress remains strong. And though other members of Congress didn't see this threat to totally

discredit Carl Albert, Tip O'Neil and Pete Rodino as early as I did, I believe it is right that no further discredit be brought upon Congress. I will have no part of it. I will not harm other people in New Jersey to buy leniency.

Three days later, on June 14, Gallagher stood before the judge in the federal court house in Newark where he was sentenced after sixty-five minutes on a first offense to two years in prison and fined $10,000 for evading $74,000 in taxes in 1966. Gallagher pleaded for "mercy and leniency" and appealed to the judge to not send him to prison, but to allow him to return to his family. He described himself as "a prisoner without chains for six years" who was subjected to more "harassment, terror and torment than any man in modern political history" as a result of his privacy war. "No man, including the prisoners of war in Vietnam, believes in the United States of America with the simplicity, trust in decency, justice and fair play more than I do," Gallagher said. He then quoted John Kenny's advice to "just do a good job."

The judge said Gallagher was treated "no better and no worse" in court than any other defendant, but that his high position of trust made him unlike other defendants. "People in the public eye must set examples," he said. "They must cut square corners. They must be like Caesar's wife." Noting that other New Jersey figures who breached the public trust were jailed for their "treasonous acts against the people," he added, "the leaders of our country should set our examples. If they do not, this should be brought home forcefully and without mitigation." The judge directed that Gallagher begin serving his prison term that Monday, when he reported to U.S. marshals in Newark to begin his two-year sentence at the federal prison camp in Allenwood, a sub-facility of the U.S. Penitentiary at Lewisburg, Pennsylvania.

Once in prison, Gallagher asserts that he was denied routine privileges granted others as a matter of course on orders that came directly from Washington. He was kept from ordinary recreational privileges; refused permission to spend his final weeks at a halfway house, though eligible for the program; and for the first eleven months of his sentence wasn't allowed a weekend furlough, though men who'd served less time were permitted the overnight visits.

Once when his baseball team was scheduled to play Bucknell College, the warden called Gallagher into his office and told him that he couldn't leave the facility on orders from Washington. The warden then told him that if he protested, he would cancel the game entirely.

His teammates caught on, however, as did Egil "Bud" Krogh, Nixon's aide in for the Watergate conspiracy, who later said during a *60 Minutes* interview with Mike Wallace that he believed Gallagher was discriminated against. "I'll be very blunt about it. Neil is a public figure with enemies in Washington. The institution here was perfectly prepared to assist him with things, but everything that's given to him or taken away is approved by Washington first and mostly it's been taken away."[2]

# XXXVI
# The Redemption

**"Hoover made it up."**

No one knows who obtained Hoover's files after his death. Some say they were shredded shortly before his death. Some say Hoover's secretary ordered them burned. Others say they wound up with Nixon. Still, whatever became of the files, Hoover was dead, his body laid out in the Rotunda of the Capitol where 25,000 people flocked to pay homage. As for Gallagher, he observed with chilly satisfaction that "25,000 people had shown up at the Capitol Rotunda to make sure the son of a bitch was really dead."

During his seventeen months of incarceration, Rick visited Gallagher regularly, often with his daughters with whom she made a game of the full-body searches. Yet, as humiliating as it must have been for her, Rick kept the family together.

On the morning of Saturday, November 23, 1974, just prior to his release, Gallagher told reporters, "I'm still deeply concerned about this one-chance society that we have. Every human action is being computerized and people believe that Congress is protecting them and taking care of their rights, but Congress isn't doing anything. In the end, the only ones who took my privacy war seriously were the law enforcement agencies. Not the people, not the Congress."

On the night of his release, he and Rick pulled up to their home and found 4,000 people overflowing the streets waiting to welcome him back. As their station wagon drew up to the back door of the house, fireworks exploded, tickertape and confetti filled the air and dozens of well-wishers swarmed the car.

Inside, trays with every type of food imaginable were placed throughout the house, prepared by the Italian, Polish, Irish and African American women of the neighborhood. Liquor flowed freely and the young men were kept busy replacing empty beer cases with full ones. It made Gallagher think back to the days of Frank Hague in the 1930s, or those of John Kenny in the 1960s, or even those of his father, Sergeant "Neil" Gallagher and Armistice Day in the mid-1920s when the entire town turned out to pay homage to the most decorated man in Bayonne.

It seemed odd to Gallagher how his family had come full circle. In the days of his father's return from World War I, they had almost nothing in the way of material wealth, but their friends and neighbors had come to their aid and didn't let them down. They kept his family from foreclosure on their home, celebrating his return as if, once again, he was returning from battle.

But now it was Rick who bore the resentment for the lies that had been spread about her by Hoover. She desperately wanted a retraction from the only other living principal who could attest to the fact that she'd been a victim as well. For nearly ten years, while he served his time in prison and struggled to make ends meet financially, she obsessed about some kind of sign, a public exoneration. Then, three months before Roy Cohn died, she got it.

Cohn was having lunch with Larry Weisman and Neil Walsh at Le Cirque when Weisman mentioned how upset Rick was. Weisman expressed to Cohn how he thought Rick would appreci-

ate something in writing from him backing up Gallagher's version
of the story, and especially a statement declaring the allegations
about her false. Walsh agreed and offered to draw a legal document
up to that effect if Cohn would agree to sign it.

"Listen," said Cohn picking a morsel of food off of Walsh's
plate as he had the habit of doing. "The whole thing was bullshit.
He wanted Gallagher and his subcommittee off their backs."

Walsh persisted and Cohn finally agreed.

> Dear Rick:
>
> I had lunch today at Le Cirque with Roy Cohn and Larry
> Weisman. In the course of the conversation, we discussed the events
> of a number of years ago concerning the articles in *Life* magazine
> about Neil. Specifically…information that Barney O'Brien had died
> in your house and his body was put in the basement and later
> removed and disposed of, and if Neil did not stop his hearings on
> invasion of privacy he would make the information public.
>
> Roy passed the information to Larry Weisman who was giv-
> ing Neil legal advice at the time, and Larry passed it along to Neil.
> That particular incident happened at Newark Airport, as I was
> there. In our conversation Roy confirmed that this is exactly what
> happened.…I thought this information would be something of great
> interest to you.
>
> Best regards.
> Sincerely,
>
> Lawrence I. Weisman
> Roy M. Cohn[1]

Two months later Cohn admitted himself into the National Institutes of Health in Bethesda, Maryland, telling close friends he'd been diagnosed with cancer of the liver. He, in fact, was being treated for HIV with the experimental drug AZT. Peter Fraser, Cohn's live-in lover, recalled Roy's final moments:

> "It was actually about ten to six, it was like his blood pressure was way down, like he'd stopped breathing and except for like every minute he would take this horrendous gasp of air. It was like he was drowning out of the water. And then one more gasp. I didn't call anybody. They came rushing in and it was like one final gasp. I was holding his hand. They dragged me out of the room and brought their equipment in and started shocking him and then, the next thing, about ten minutes later, I saw this covered bed wheeled out the door?"[2]

Cohn died on July 22, 1986. Such was the hatred he inspired among some that soon after his death, one man went around New York City's Greenwich Village boasting that he'd arranged for Cohn to catch his death by pairing him with an infected lover. For his part, despite all that happened, Gallagher bore no grudge against the man.

# XXXVII
# The Raid

### Columbia, N.J., February 6, 1992

The sound of FBI, DEA and IRS agents converged around him. The radio blared "No Fences" by Garth Brooks while in the other room Rick and the grandkids listened to the singsong melodies of Raffi on the VCR. The special agent still presided over the bedlam.

One of the DEA agents returning from the living room, which was now torn apart, approached the special agent, who stood surveying the chaos. "Nothing here, boss," he said shaking his head in frustration. "No drugs. No firearms. Your IRS guys have been through his office. They got a pile of paper. That's it."

The special agent nodded. "Good enough. Let's get out of here." He then turned to the foot of the staircase where Gallagher sat, head in hands, visibly shaken. "We're going to call it a day, Neil. Like they say in Hudson County government from 11:00 to 11:30, no heavy lifting. You remember that, don't you, Neil, Hudson County government, because we sure do." He swiveled around and called out to the fifty others who populated the three floors of their family dwelling. "Check with the others to see where they are," he ordered a female officer in the kitchen, holding a two-way radio. "If they're done, we call it a day."

The woman initiated communication with agents at the two other residences of the complex where Gallagher's children lived, which were subjected to simultaneous raids.

The FBI, DEA and ATF agents began leaving the house, which was now ransacked, while others carried out crates of Gallagher's paperwork, computer disks and financial journals from his home office.

Gallagher raised his head. "Rick." he shouted at the top of his lungs. "Your mother. Have you checked on her? Is she all right?"

"Okay," the special agent bade. "We're out of here."

"Rick. You check on her." he called out in a ringing voice. "I'll stay with the kids." He turned to the agent. "You better hope your people were on their best behavior today because I swear if one of them touched my daughters or their kids, I'm coming after you."

"No need to worry about my people, Congressman. Read your warrant. Mail fraud, conspiracy, bank fraud, money laundering, I'd say that should give you plenty to think about."

"So what is all this? Are madmen running the government now?"

"This much I can tell you: There are a lot of people spending time looking into you and your family."

"There is no Gallagher organization, and you know it. I don't know exactly what you think you know, but I promise you, I'm going to find out."

"Maybe sooner, rather than later," the agent promised.

And with that, the siege was over. The only sound left was the music of Raffi.

"You guys okay?" Gallagher asked.

His grandchildren nodded. He then looked through the window that overlooked the entrance to their compound to see three, then five and soon the dozen or more unmarked cars and vans pull away down the long dirt road that led to Route 94.

Rick ambled down the staircase into the den where the children and he waited, vigilantly surveying the shambles they'd been left with. "Mom's doing fine. A little shaken is all. I promised I'd make her some tea."

"I'm going to check on the girls."

"I called, Neil. They're good. Just trying to clean up the mess after all of this."

"I'm checking on them anyway. I want to see for myself."

"Whatever you say," Rick soothed.

Within minutes, they all gathered from each of the three houses in the kitchen.

"Look, let me get on the phone with Ray Brown," Gallagher said. "He knows people in the prosecutor's office and can find out what's behind all of this nonsense. On a worst case basis, we'll turn something up through the Freedom of Information Act. It might take a while, but for all of their searching and accusations there's nothing anybody's found in this house, or yours, that can hurt us. For now, anyway, it's just a piece of paper."

But as Gallagher was to discover, it was not just a piece of paper. It was a warrant that, through the Freedom of Information Act, he later learned was based on a pervasive investigation, not only of him, but of most of his family members, that went back at least nine years to August 1983. The information was obtained through a copy of the application for permission to wiretap his office and residence phones in Columbia, N.J. Dated November 23, 1984, it identified him as a high-profile "target" for the president's Organized Crime Drug Enforcement Investigation program and, at that time, involved agents and resources from the FBI, IRS, ATF and DEA. On January 30, 1985, wiretaps and surveillance were authorized of his entire family.

In a subsequent application for the creation of a multi-agency "strike force" to carry forward the investigation, approved March 20, 1985, there were allegations of international drug trafficking and money laundering involving contacts in the Middle East and Colombia.

The message, to Gallagher, rang as clear and ominous as the toll of a death knell. Most, if not all, of his immediate family and he had been under government surveillance, with their phones wiretapped. Calculating from the 1960s when his Privacy Hearings began when he was first warned by many about surveillance on his residence and congressional office, Gallagher would have thirty years of intensive probing into his professional life and private affairs. This was more time than spent on many of the men and women who committed espionage during the Cold War.

For many nights after the February 6, 1992, raid on his home, Gallagher could not sleep and would often wander through the house as if looking for something, but didn't know what it could be. He would devour newspapers, sometimes ten a day, along with magazines and books, mostly related to the founding of the FBI and CIA or their current activities. Television, too, was a pastime, and he made a habit of viewing international news broadcasts via a satellite dish he'd had installed at their home. It was during one of these late nights in mid-March that Rick joined him for a cup of coffee in their kitchen.

"I've had discussions with Ray Brown and even called Ramsey Clark for advice," he told her. "But once your name gets put into this prosecution machine, there's little you can do to stop it."

On April 19, 1996 Gallagher plead guilty to charges of federal conspiracy to commit fraud and income tax evasion for failing to report $90,000 earned in 1989 on the sale of a condominium

Rick and he owned in the Dominican Republic. Since Gallagher couldn't leave the country as a condition of his parole, he was not personally involved in the sale by check, which he understood to be a wash, returning no income after legal fees, commissions and local taxes. As it turned out, the transaction was done with checks as well as cash that Gallagher maintains he knew nothing about and never received.

The following morning, Gallagher stated before the U.S. District judge, "I accept full responsibility for the reasons I am here today. I never did anything against anybody except try to give them hope or help them. I tried to deal honestly with everybody I knew."

Despite his pleas, on May 28, 1996, with Rick and his daughters at his side, Gallagher was committed to Schuylkill Federal Penitentiary. Ray Brown characterized the congressman's fall from grace as an "American tragedy."

# EPILOGUE

Today, Neil Gallagher is philosophical about the issues that so obsessed him back in the 1960s and '70s. That isn't because he cares less about them, but because the issues of privacy and civil liberties are no longer just his war. Seventy-nine years old at the time of this writing, this book is, to him, the only medium left to alert people about what the United States of America was then and could someday become again.

"I'm not sure how it will come out, but I believe that our democratic form of government is most threatened during times of war or perceived crisis, especially now given recent technological breakthroughs," Gallagher said in an interview ten months before the terrorist attacks on the Pentagon and World Trade Center. Still, his accounts of pervasive governmental abuse of the rights of U.S. citizens during the Cold War period must resonate within our minds and hearts today.

Most late 20th-century attempts to forecast future threats failed to recall Winston Churchill's dictum that before attempting to look forward, one must first look a long way back. There are, however, some striking exceptions. Perhaps, the most notable was the warning given by Elie Wiesel, Holocaust survivor and human rights activist, to a conference in New York. "The principle challenge of the 21st century," Wiesel said, "will be exactly the same as the principle challenge of the 20th century: How do we deal with fanaticism armed with power?"

Locating and analyzing the threat from "fanaticism armed with power" is the greatest challenge facing strategic intelligence. Those who did most damage during the 20th century were fanatics armed with power: Hitler, Stalin, Mao Zedong and Pol Pot chief among them. Those who will do most damage during the 21st century will also be fanatics armed with power, but we will need to deal with a different kind of fanatic.

In the year 2002, the major threat to U.S. security is not Nazism, socialism or Communism, but terrorism. The names are also new: Shoko Asahara, leader of the Japanese cult Aum Shinrikyo, who launched a nerve gas attack on the Tokyo subway in 1995; Timothy McVeigh, found guilty of the Oklahoma City bombing; and Osama bin Laden, who masterminded the World Trade Center and Pentagon attacks and has told his followers, "We are not fighting so the enemy will offer us something. We are fighting to wipe out the enemy."

These are insidious words, Gallagher believes, spoken by evil men who represent not only a formidable challenge to United States security, but to the nation's democratic way of life. Predictably, after this most recent declaration of war, the rush to defend the country by any means necessary has cleared the way for a raft of controversial technologies including Internet wiretaps, online video cameras, DNA profiling, and face-recognition and fingerprint-scanning devices. Longstanding policies that protect the individual rights of citizens are also being challenged.

Gallagher alerts us to the fact that Attorney General John Ashcroft has asked for expanded rights to conduct computer and telephone wiretaps to "identify, prevent and punish terrorism."[1] Senator Orrin Hatch has proposed an amendment that allows any U.S. attorney to authorize the installation of "trap and trace" equipment for up to forty-eight hours.[2] The FBI's Carnivore system, renamed DC1000 for the sake of public palatability, once questioned by conservative Republicans like Rep. Dick Armey, today goes unchallenged as it sorts through all e-mail correspondence between law-abiding American citizens traveling over any Internet service provider. In an unprecedented move, the National Security Agency invoked attorney-client privilege in blocking last year's congressional inquiry into the Echelon satellite spy system, but now that inquiry has been dropped entirely. On September 17, 2001, Senate Intelligence Committee chairman Bob Graham of Florida agreed to review lifting the two-decade-old executive order banning the assassination of foreign leaders. [3]

In all of these cases, it would do us well to remember why many of these restrictions were put into place. It wasn't because of foreign abuses of wiretaps, surveillance and black bag jobs carried out in the homes of American citizens, but rather abuses by our own federal agencies. A modicum of skepticism may also be in order before giving carte blanche to federal law enforcement with regard to "trap and trace" equipment, DNA profiling and a renewed policy allowing assassination of foreign leaders. After all, it was J. Edgar Hoover who allegedly used personal data gathered through illegal surveillance to blackmail, "neutralize" and imprison unsuspecting American citizens and their representatives in Congress. DNA profiling, too, while nearly a foolproof way of identifying would-be terrorists could also be used by nefarious leaders and their subordinate agencies to frame innocent men and women targeted for political persecution.

If Gallagher is correct in interpreting the now-available evidence regarding the Kennedy and King assassinations, the executive order barring the assassination of foreign leaders may well have been ratified not because of the hundreds of assassinations perpetrated by the CIA on foreign soil, but because of their complicity in executions performed on domestic soil, in the United States. So it seems we are compelled to follow Winston Churchill's dictum because Gallagher's missing piece of history tells us much about our government and a lot about ourselves.

Gallagher believes we are still faced with real threats to our national security. The genius of our Constitution is that it is flexible enough to incorporate reason into its limits. What is reasonable must be taken into account. But before we surrender personal liberty for national security, we would be wise to ask: To whom is this authority going? Will America ever be as free again? Because in the end, Gallagher concludes, the largest international terrorist agency over the last half century has not been the foreign organizations that the United States intelligence agencies have targeted, but the United States intelligence agencies themselves.

# NOTES

## Foreword

1. This information has been gathered from taped interviews between Felber and Gallagher conducted from December 1998 to June 1999. All subsequent information taken from Felber's interviews with Gallagher are not footnoted.

2. Summers, Anthony, *Official and Confidential: The Secret Life of J. Edgar Hoover*. (New York: G. P. Putnam, 1994), p. 241.

## Chapter 1

1. *Star-Ledger*, March 11, 1989.

## Chapter 2

1. *Jersey Journal*, October 24, 1954.

2. Doherty, Jane, *Hudson County, The Left Bank*. (New York: Random House, 1953), pp. 111-112.

3. Reeves, Thomas C., *A Question of Character: A Life of John F. Kennedy*. (New York: Macmillan, 1991), pp. 153-154.

## Chapter 3

1. Von Hoffman, Nicholas, *Citizen Cohn: The Life and Times of Roy*

*Cohn*, (New York: Doubleday, 1988), p. 395.

## Chapter 6

1. Reeves, *A Question of Character: A Life of John F. Kennedy*, p. 165.

2. Ibid.

3. Summers, *Official and Confidential: The Secret Life of J. Edgar Hoover*, p. 311.

4. Bonanno interview with Felber.

5. Ibid.

## Chapter 7

1.*Life*, October 7, 1967. ©1967 TIME, Inc. Reprinted by permission.

## Chapter 8

1. Reeves, *A Question of Character: A Life of John F. Kennedy*, pp. 169-170.

2. Ibid., p. 171.

## Chapter 9

1. Summers, *Official and Confidential: The Secret Life of J. Edgar Hoover*, 314.

2. Ibid., p. 337.

3. Reeves, *A Question of Character: A Life of John F. Kennedy*, p. 199.

4. *Newark Evening News*, May 23, 1961.

## Chapter 11
1. Marks, John. *In Search of the Manchurian Candidate*, (New York: Times Books, 1979), pp. 173-174.

2. Ibid., pp. 178-179.

3. Rosenberg, Jerry M., *The Death of Privacy*, (New York: Random House, 1969), p. 163.

## Chapter 12
1. *New York Daily Mirror*, October 13, 1962.

2. May, Ernest R., and Philip D. Zelikow, *The Kennedy Tapes: Inside the White House During the Cuban Missile Crisis*, (Cambridge: Harvard University Press, 1997), p. 43.

3. Reeves, *A Question of Character: A Life of John F. Kennedy*, p. 376.

## Chapter 13
1. Summers, *Official and Confidential: The Secret Life of J. Edgar Hoover*, pp. 328-329.

2. *Washington Post*, October 13, 1963.

3. Summers, *Official and Confidential: The Secret Life of J. Edgar Hoover*, p. 358.

4. Ibid., pp. 363-364.

5. Mailer, Norman. *The Time of our Time*, (New York: Random House, 1998), p. 356.

6. Reeves, *A Question of Character: A Life of John F. Kennedy*, p. 400.

7. Commager, Lawrence. *John Fitzgerald Kennedy*, (New York: Doubleday, 1972), 93.

## Chapter 14

1. Gentry, Curt. *J. Edgar Hoover, The Man and the Secrets*, (New York: W. W. Norton & Co., 1991), p. 547.

2. Ibid.

3. Ibid., 548.

4. Summers, *Official and Confidential: The Secret Life of J. Edgar Hoover*, p. 367.

## Chapter 15

1. House of Representatives, Congressional Record, Gallagher Privacy Subcommittee, September 8, 1964.

## Chapter 16

1. Marks, *In Search of the Manchurian Candidate*, p. 211.

2. Ibid., p. 184.

3. Ibid., p. 183.

4. Ibid., p. 185.

5. Bechloss, Michael R. *Taking Charge: The Johnson White House Tapes, 1963-1964*, (New York: Simon & Schuster, 1997), p. 58.

6. Lawrence, Lincoln and Kenn Thomas. *Mind Control, Oswald and JFK: Were We Controlled?*, (Chicago: Adventures Unlimited Press, 1967), pp. 58-58.

## Chapter 17

1. *Washington Sun-Sentinel*, June 22, 1965.

2. Ibid.

3. Ibid.

4. MORI ID 70520:70520, Jones.

5. MORI ID 70520:70520, Jones.

6. MORI ID 70520:70520, Jones.

7. MORI ID 70520:70520, Jones.

8. Schulman, Bruce J. *Lyndon B. Johnson and American Liberalism*, (New York: St. Martin's Press, 1995), p. 137.

## Chapter 19

1. Minnesota Multi-Phasic Index (MMPI): House of Representatives, Special Inquiry on Invasion of Privacy, September 23, 1965, pp. 167-169.

2. Ibid., p. 171.

3. Ibid., p. 169.

4. Ibid., p. 193.

5. Ibid., p. 197.

## Chapter 20

1. Gentry, *J. Edgar Hoover, The Man and the Secrets*, pp. 442-445.

2. Ibid.

## Chapter 21

1. Schulman, *Lyndon B. Johnson and American Liberalism*, pp. 100-101.

2. Mailer, Norman. *Harlot's Ghost*, (New York: Random House, 1991), p. 716.

3. Heyman, David C. *RFK: A Candid Biography of Robert F. Kennedy*, (New York: Dutton, 1998), pp. 357-358.

4. Ibid.

## Chapter 22

1. *Life*, September 1, 1967. ©1967 TIME, Inc. Reprinted by permission.

2. Ibid., October 7, 1967.

3. Ibid.

## Chapter 23

1. Gallagher Interview with Felber.

2. *Napa Sentinel*, October 22, 1991.

3. Committee on Government Operations, Privacy and the National Data Bank Concept, U.S. Government Printing Office, July 1968.

4. *Des Moines Register*, February 12, 1967.

5. Committee on Government Operations, Gallagher Privacy Bill, February 8, 1972.

6. Ibid.

7. Speech given at the American Bar Association Convention, "Technology and Freedom," February 14, 1967.

8. Zwick letter to Johnson, March 3, 1967.

## Chapter 24

1. Gentry, *J. Edgar Hoover, The Man and the Secrets*, p. 568.

2. Summers, *Official and Confidential: The Secret Life of J. Edgar Hoover*, pp. 343-344.

3. Ibid.

4. Ibid.

## Chapter 25

1. Committee on Government Operations, 1970 Census Questions, August 25, 1966.

2. Ibid.

3. Harris, Robert and Jeremy Paxman, *A Higher Form of Killing*, (New York: Noonday Press, 1982), pp. 240-241.

4. Committee on Government Operations, Gallagher Privacy Bill, February 8, 1972.

5. Huie, William Bradford. *He Slew The Dreamer: My Search, With James Earl Ray, for the Truth About the Murder of Martin Luther King, Jr.*, (Montgomery, Alabama: Black Belt Press, 1997), p. 184.

6. Mailer, Norman. *Oswald's Tale: An American Mystery*, (New York: Random House, 1993), p. 671.

7. Lawrence and Thomas, *Mind Control, Oswald and JFK: Were We Controlled?*, pp. 101.

8. Klaber, William and Philip H. Melanson, *Shadow Play: The Untold Story of the Robert F. Kennedy Assassination*, (New York: St. Martin's Press, 1998), p. 184.

9. Ibid., p. 186.

10. Lawrence and Lawrence, *Mind Control, Oswald and JFK: Were We Controlled?*, p. 106.

11. Huie, *He Slew The Dreamer: My Search, With James Earl Ray, for the Truth About the Murder of Martin Luther King, Jr.*, p. 187.

12. Klaber and Melanson, *Shadow Play: The Untold Story of the Robert F. Kennedy Assassination*, p. 203.

13. Mailer, *Oswald's Tale: An American Mystery*, 357.

14. Huie, *He Slew The Dreamer: My Search, With James Earl Ray, for the Truth About the Murder of Martin Luther King, Jr.*, p. 193.

15. Klaber and Melanson, *Shadow Play: The Untold Story of the Robert F. Kennedy Assassination*, p. 206.

16. Marks, *In Search of the Manchurian Candidate*, p. 193.

## Chapter 26

1. *Star-Ledger*, August 2, 1968.

2. *Jersey Journal*, August 7, 1968.

3. *New York Times*, August 8, 1968.

4. *Morning Call*, August 19, 1968.

## Chapter 27

1. Congressional Record, Gallagher Details Link Between FBI and Life Magazine, April 19, 1972.

2. *New York Times*, August 15, 1968.

3. Ibid.

4. *Life*, August 30, 1968. ©1968 TIME, Inc. Reprinted by permission.

5. *Life*, September 7, 1968. ©1968 TIME, Inc. Reprinted by permission.

6. *Life*, October 21, 1968. ©1968 TIME, Inc. Reprinted by permission.

## Chapter 28

1. *Bayonne Times*, December 14, 1968.

2. Summers, Anthony, *The Arrogance of Power*, (New York: Viking, 2000), pp. 60-80.

3 Ibid.

4 Emery, Fred, *Watergate: The Corruption of American Politics and the Fall of Richard Nixon*, (New York: Simon & Schuster, 1995), pp. 25-27.

## Chapter 29

1. Congressional Record, The Return of Lobotomy and

Psychosurgery, April 14, 1970.

2. Ibid.

3. Ibid.

4. Marks, *In Search of the Manchurian Candidate*, pp. 214.

5. Committee on Government Operations, Federal Involvement In The Use of Behavior Modification Drugs on Grammar School Children, 1972.

6. Committee on Government Operations, STARR Program: Federal Involvement in the Use of Behavior Modification Drugs on Grammar School Children, September 29, 1970.

## Chapter 30

1. *Jersey Journal*, June 28, 1969.

2. Ibid.

3. Ibid.

4. Department of Treasury, File # 15-48-8226.

5. *Newsweek*, July 27, 1970. ©1970 Newsweek, Inc. All rights reserved. Reprinted by permission.

## Chapter 31

1. *Elizabeth Daily Journal*, May 8, 1969.

2. Harris and Packman, *A Higher Form of Killing*, pp. 240-241.

3. Ibid., pp. 206-207.

4. Marks, *In Search of the Manchurian Candidate*, p. 203.

5. Ibid., p. 207.

6. Ibid., p. 194.

7. *Newsweek*, May 7, 1984. ©1984 Newsweek, Inc. All rights reserved. Reprinted by permission.

8. Cantwell, Jr., Alan, M.D., *AIDS and the Doctors of Death*, (Los Angeles: Aries Rising Press, 1987), p. 182.

9. *Journal of the Royal Society of Medicine*, August 1986.

10. *London Times*, May 11, 1987.

## Chapter 32

1. *Washington Post*, September 22, 1971.

2. Summers, *Official and Confidential: The Secret Life of J. Edgar Hoover*, p. 430.

3. Klaber and Melanson, *Shadow Play: The Untold Story of the Robert F. Kennedy Assassination*, pp. 107-108.

4. Gentry, *J. Edgar Hoover, The Man and the Secrets*, 382-385.

5. Bonanno interview with Felber.

## Chapter 34

1. *New York Post*, April 1971.

## Chapter 35

1. *New York Daily News*, June 9, 1972.

2. Summers, *Official and Confidential: The Secret Life of J. Edgar Hoover*, pp. 479-480.

## Chapter 36

1. Lawrence Weisman/Roy Cohn Document, April 24, 1986.

2. Von Hoffman, *Citizen Cohn: The Life and Times of Roy Cohn*, pp. 35-40.

## EPILOGUE

1. *The Economist*, "Government and Civil Liberties," September 29, 2001.

2. *USA Today*, "Beware of Simple Solutions," October 22, 2001.

3. *USA Today*, September 18, 2001.

# BIBLIOGRAPHY

Anderson, Jon Lee. *Che Guevara, A Revolutionary Life*. New York: Grove Press, 1997.

Bechloss, Michael R. *Taking Charge: The Johnson White House Tapes, 1963-1964*. New York: Simon & Schuster, 1997.

Bernstein, Carl, and Bob Woodward. *All the President's Men*. New York: Warner Books, 1975.

Bonanno, Bill. *Bound By Honor: A Mafioso's Story*. New York: St. Martin's Press, 1999.

Cantwell, Alan, Jr., M.D. *AIDS And the Doctors of Death: An Inquiry into the Origin of the AIDS Epidemic*. Los Angeles: Aries Rising Press, 1987.

Cole, Leonard A. *Clouds of Secrecy*. Baltimore: Rowman and Littlefield, 1990.

Commercial Credit Bureaus. Washington, D.C.: U.S. Government Printing Office, 1968.

Emery, Fred. *Watergate: The Corruption of American Politics and the Fall of Richard Nixon*. New York: Simon & Schuster, 1995.

Gentry, Curt. *J. Edgar Hoover: The Man and the Secrets*. New York: W.W. Norton, 1991.

Halberstein, David. *The Best and the Brightest*. New York: Random House, 1972.

Harris, Robert, and Jeremy Paxman. *A Higher Form of Killing*. New York: Noonday Press, 1982.

Huie, William Bradford. *He Slew The Dreamer: My Search, With James Earl Ray, for the Truth About the Murder of Martin Luther King, Jr.* Montgomery, AL: Black Belt Press, 1997.

Heymann, David C. *RFK: A Candid Biography of Robert F. Kennedy*. New York: Dutton, 1998.

Jones, James H. *Bad Blood: The Tuskegee Syphilis Experiment*. New York: The Free Press, 1981.

Kafka, Franz. *The Trial*. New York: Shocken Books, 1961.

Klaber, William, and Philip H. Melanson. *Shadow Play: The Untold Story of the Robert F. Kennedy Assassination*. New York: St. Martin's Press, 1998.

Knightley, Philip. *The Master Spy: The Story of Kim Philby*. New York: Alfred A. Knopf, 1989.

Liddy, G. Gordon. *Will*. New York: St. Martin's Press, 1980.

Livingston, Harrison Edward. *High Treason 2: The Great Cover-Up: The Assassination of President John F. Kennedy*. New York: Carroll & Graf, 1992.

Mailer, Norman. *Harlot's Ghost*. New York: Random House, 1991.

Mailer, Norman. *Oswald's Tale: An American Mystery*. New York: Random House, 1993.

Marks, John. *In Search of the Manchurian Candidate*. New York: Times Books, 1979.

May, Ernest R., and Philip D. Zelikow. *The Kennedy Tapes: Inside the White House During the Cuban Missile Crisis*. Cambridge, MA: Harvard Press, 1997.

Nash, Jay Robert. *Citizen Hoover: A Critical Study of the Life and Times of J. Edgar Hoover and His FBI*. Chicago: Nelson Hall, 1972.

Partmet, Herbert S. *Jack: The Struggles of John F. Kennedy*. New York: Dial Press, 1983.

Reeves, Thomas C. *A Question of Character: A Life of John F. Kennedy*. New York: Macmillan, 1991.

Rosenberg, Jerry M., *The Death of Privacy*. New York: Random House, 1969.

Schulman, Bruce J. *Lyndon B. Johnson and American Liberalism: A Brief Biography with Documents*. New York: St. Martin's Press, 1995.

Skinner, B. F. *Beyond Freedom and Dignity*. New York: Vintage Books, 1971.

Summers, Anthony. *The Arrogance of Power*. New York: Viking, 2000.

Summers, Anthony. *Official and Confidential: The Secret Life of J. Edgar Hoover*. New York: G. P. Putnam, 1994.

Lawrence, Lincoln, and Kenn Thomas. *Mind Control, Oswald and JFK: Were We Controlled?*. Chicago: Adventures Unlimited Press, 1967.

U.S. Government Printing Office. Federal Involvement in the Use of Behavior Modification Drugs on Grammar School Children. Washington, D.C.: 1970.

U.S. Government Printing Office. Gallagher Privacy Bill. Washington, D.C.:, 1972.

U.S. Government Printing Office. Privacy and the National Data Bank Concept. Washington, D.C.: 1968.

U.S. Government Printing Office. Special Inquiry on Invasion of Privacy. Washington, D.C.: 1966.

U.S. Government Printing Office. Use of Polygraphs by the Federal Government. Washington, D.C.: 1964.

Von Hoffman, Nicholas. *Citizen Cohn: The Life and Times of Roy Cohn*. New York: Doubleday, 1988.

Ziegler, Henry A. *The New Jersey Mob*. New York: New American
Library, 1975.

# THE PRIVACY WAR

# INDEX

**295**